THE NEW NOW

Grow your production or postproduction business in a changed and changing world

THE NEW NOW

Grow your production or postproduction business in a changed and changing world

PHILIP HODGETTS

Intelligent Assistance, Inc,
Burbank California

Contents

The New Now... 1

    Introduction   1

    Marketing using the "new PR" and social conversations 4

    Owning your own content   5

The number one thing you should do, and do it now...... 7

    Contact your clients   7

    If you get a meeting   7

    You won't be the only one   8

What business are you in?..11

    It's the talent, not the tools   12

    Focus on the Unique Selling Proposition, not the
marketplace   12

Clarify your Brand.. 15

    Developing your brand   16

    Make your world smaller   17

    Double your prices!   17

Expand into new areas... 21

    Learn new skills   21

    Expand Geographically   24

    Partner with other business or add services   27

Marketing, PR and Social conversations......................... 29

New PR is being part of the conversation.   30

Marketing is storytelling   31

Think like a the media outlet   38

The pitch letter   40

Be and know Influencers   42

Network   46

Social Media   47

Be part of the conversation   50

Lead a Tribe   52

Why you should have a business blog........................... 55

You'll be great   56

Blogging Tips   58

Maximize your visibility on the Internet.......................... 67

Install Google Analytics   69

Search Engine Optimization   70

Other traffic building tips   78

Six Little Words   84

Use YouTube (etc.) as your calling card   85

Sell.. 89

What you need before you get more customers   89

Turn into a great salesperson   90

How to be more persuasive   92

Display advertising vs Search advertising 93

Adsense, Adwords 94

Cut Costs.. 99

Open Source or inexpensive Software 100

Virtual Offices 107

Cheaper Hosting 108

Review printing costs 110

Use Free Resources 111

Work smarter...113

Search the Internet 113

How to Produce More Cheaply 119

Get Paid Faster 139

Find your own income... 145

The value of owning content 147

The New Now

1:   The New Now

If you've been paying attention to your business lately, you'll know customers think cheaper equipment should lead to cheaper production; that the proverbial 'kid in a basement' underbids at every turn; that many traditional sources of production revenue are simply drying up; and distribution is moving to the Internet. These trends were happening, but an economic downturn has accelerated the changes. The Internet has radically changed communication and, fortunately, brought us powerful new tools for communicating the benefits your company provides. This is the New Now – the new business reality – with new opportunities and new ways of growing your business, whatever the economic conditions.

Introduction

There is no doubt that we are living in changed, and changing, economic times. While the worldwide economic downturn has accelerated changes already happening, we are heading into a "New Now" – a time when most of the rules of engagement in business, with customers and with the world is changing, almost constantly.

Get used to living in a world where change is the new constant. Not that you haven't dealt with change before: from tape to digital; from linear to non-linear; from VHS to DVD to online distribution; from higher to lower budgets; and from SD to HD. If you've stayed in the production or postproduction business for more than a few years, you've already weathered significant change.

This book is about weathering the current change. Not only surviving but thriving and growing in changed circumstances.

Back in December 2008, I heard an interview[1] where the guest summed up what you need to do to survive in business in the New Now: project stability and provide great value. To that I'd want to add: "work smarter." Those three points summarize the advice in this book.

---

[1] Dec 22 Money 101 interview KNX1070 Los Angeles

In that radio interview the guest acknowledged the obvious dilemma: in a downturn, business slows so there's less money to spend on marketing. How can you market if you're worried about making payroll? In reality, the one activity you can't afford to stop is marketing.

Projecting stability

You exhibit stability through your brand: the values your business stands for that govern how you do business. This is presumably the reason why your clients hire you.

Part of your value is your stability. Unlike low-priced newcomers you bring experience and business continuity to the table. You need to make these a key part of your business story.

Projecting stability becomes part of your marketing message. This is not the time to suddenly move office; redecorate or change the way you produce. Clients look for continuity – the same service, the same location, the same people – when they look for stability.

Providing great value

We shouldn't just be focused on surviving. A recession/depression/downturn – changed circumstances that are continually changing, what we call the New Now – is a great opportunity to build your business. It's a time to assess: where do you provide the most value for your current and potential customers?

To do that you'll need to assess just what business you are in. Chances are you'll find it isn't the one you're currently marketing. You'll also need to clarify your brand: the statement of who you are and how you do business that permeates every aspect of your business.

These are essential starting points, but by themselves they won't help you grow the business. It will help you determine how you'll go about it.

Working smarter

The production business has always been based on teams that come together for a project, then take their expertise to the next project, but not necessarily with the same team. Find the right partner businesses and you can both grow faster together than either can alone. I know from "enjoying" the opposite experience back in Australia, where four fledgling competitors in a small market ultimately opted not to join forces. The result was that that we all remained small scale competitors.

Should you take this time to develop and extend your own skills – to offer more services to your current clients or expand into new areas? A quieter period of business is a great opportunity to become more familiar with your existing software tools, or explore ways to work more efficiently. Working more efficiently transmits directly to profitability. Bill the same, and do the work faster giving you an effectively higher rate; or lower your rate, do the job faster and get the same net return for the job. Either way, you're getting more for every hour you spend working. (It's time to consider project-based fees instead of an hourly rate when you become significantly more efficient than your peers or competitors.)

When you think about expanding into new areas, think both literally and metaphorically. It's a new age and there are a lot of services that can be offered to customers outside your local geographic area. Thanks to the Internet, FedEx/UPS and the telephone, there are many practitioners who haven't ever met their best clients.

Given that profit is the bit you get to keep between what your customers pay and what you have to spend, you'll want consider ways that costs can be cut, without reducing the quality of the services you use, or provide. From using open source software instead of the commercial versions, to cheaper hosting, virtual offices, printing costs and more, there are ways to reduce your costs.

Marketing using the "new PR" and social conversations

You keep business coming through the door by marketing. Marketing is not advertising. Marketing is every interaction your business has with the customer. It includes the look and comfort of your offices or lack thereof, the way you and your staff dress, how tidy your spaces are, promptness, competence, etc. What form these take depends on the values of your brand.

Marketing is the message you send at every interaction. Advertising is the way that you let people know you even exist as a solution to their problem. Once you had to spend a lot on ads in newspapers, magazines, Yellow (or Pink) Pages advertising, brochures, flyers... Bigger businesses hired Public Relations (PR) companies to, essentially, buy them exposure. Good PR Agents would bring relevant stories to the attention of media associates they knew, garnering coverage.

Then along came the Internet. There are many more ways to get your message out there by optimizing for search engines and by doing your own "new PR" – PR for those with the story to tell.

All PR and Media relations are about having an interesting story to tell, and tell it to those who have audiences that would be interested in hearing about it. There aren't the same barriers of access to audiences as there used to be, when some blogs have higher readership than many (failing) newspapers. Some of these are more likely to be catering to your customer niche directly where your stories are interesting to their audiences. A positive review of a Final Cut Studio training product at KenStone.net (for example) has a direct effect on sales and on getting the word out. Ken's site only caters to Final Cut Studio users, and they get high quality relevant content.

PR doesn't have the same high cost it once did. A combination of good, modern internet-focused marketing, good networking skills in your local community, and search engine optimization can bring in better results than expensive traditional advertising – for fewer dollars and a little bit of time.

This is the change of the New Now: marketing, communication and conversation with your current and prospective customers are built on social media concepts. Communication is not one way, but a conversation where customers matter as much as the company.

Owning your own content

Finally, own some content. A few years back everyone trying to break into the business in Los Angeles (a.k.a. "Hollywood") had a screenplay. These days they have a web series as a calling card.

Producers and directors are realizing that keeping control of (i.e. owning) their content gives them many more revenue opportunities. Certainly my experience is that owning content, and selling it multiple times over, is a great way to smooth over business-cycle ups and downs.

But before we get to that, there's one thing you should be doing now, and that's coming right up.

Further reading

Ten Rules for the New Economy [2] from the perspective of a customer-focused lawyer.

Staying Afloat in the Stupid Economy [3] – Studio Daily asks industry practitioners how they plan to stay afloat in the changing economy.

Business Advice for Tough Times [4] brings the summary of wisdom from CreativeCow.net's business forums.

Winning in Turbulence: What Does the Downturn Mean for My Business and How Will I Get Through It?) [5] from Memo to the CEO column in the Harvard Business Review.

Winning in Turbulence: How to Turbo Charge Sales [6] – Second post from Memo to the CEO column in the Harvard Business Review.

---

[2] http://thenonbillablehour.typepad.com/nonbillable_hour/2008/12/ten-rules-for-t.html

[3] http://www.studiodaily.com/main/news/10499.html

[4] http://library.creativecow.net/articles/cowdog/its_all_your_fault.php

[5] http://ceomemo.harvardbusiness.org/2008/12/winning_in_turbulence_what_doe.html

[6] http://ceomemo.harvardbusiness.org/2008/12/bain_post_2.html

2: The number one thing you should do, and do it now

Contact your clients

Call them, write to them, send an email – whatever way you contact your past and present customers, contact them. Don't commiserate about how bad the economy is. Don't complain and moan how quiet business is, simply ask if there's anything you can do to help. As Seth Godin says[7] contact them along these lines:

> "I know that times might be tough for you. Is there anything I can do to pitch in and help?"

Listen, and then do it. Even for nothing if it's a small thing that you can do to help. Just the fact that you're listening and asking will score you some karma points for the future.

If you get a meeting

If, as a result of asking, one of your clients wants to "talk" in a meeting, remember that there's nothing different in this economic climate than any other: you need to add more value to the client's business than you cost.

Know your client

Before the meeting learn as much as you can about the client. Feel free to share your "war stories" but be very careful to keep the meeting about the client. Learn as much as you can about their business: read through their website and spend a few minutes Googling the client company and contacts.

Know what you don't know

Even if you're well researched, arrive with a curious attitude and lots of questions. People instinctively like people who are interested in them.

---

[7] http://sethgodin.typepad.com/seths_blog/2009/01/easiest-cheap-w.html

Keep your eyes and ears open for any little clues in your client group during a presentation or the meeting. If you see a reaction among one or more people to the point you're discussing, follow up on that point with a question, to discover the client's agenda on the subject. Being able to think on your feet and move toward the client's need in the presentation shows that you listen and can be flexible – highly desirable traits in a contractor.

You won't be the only one

You can almost guarantee that you won't be the only person contacting, or presenting to, your clients. Every other production or post production business in your area will likely be calling, as well as any new entrant to the business who might be prepared to undercut to get started.

Whether or not you get the meeting, or the job, will depend on the sort of relationship you've had with your client in the past, and how well you can articulate to the client the value that you bring in specific terms.

Most of your competition are going into these meetings focused on their need to stay in business. No doubt that's in your mind to, but it can never be the focus of your presentation. There is only one thing the client is interested in: how you're going to help them make more money. Keep that clearly in mind and the total focus of what you present.

Also, be very clear <u>what business you are in</u>. It probably isn't the one you think it is.

Sell more to your existing customers

Keeping clients is always less expensive than finding new ones. Selling more to today's clients is even better. Think McDonalds and offer additional, relevant services.

Delight them with little extra touches. Back in the days when graphic design was expensive, we would attempt to delight our customers by providing a high quality, well-designed slick and label for their tape covers, and later, DVD slicks. DVDs were always provided in solid cases, with a slick, and never in a cheap paper or Kevlar pocket.

Serve your clients well. Listen to them, understand their needs and use that information to suggest extra services you might perform for them that will move them closer to their business goals.

Understand your client's perceptions. You won't be able to astound them with your great service if you don't know what their definition of great service actually is. When you know it, do it!

Make Special rules for your best customers

There's no doubt that people like to be made to feel special. When people get something extra they weren't expecting, they respond very positively. So find some extra services, gifts or special way of treating your best customers. Perhaps provide them with free meals during edits (unless you do that for everyone) or do additional dubs at cost (or free). You know what will work for your business better than anyone so:

Identify your best customers. What you'll probably find is that a relatively small group of your customers bring in the majority of the income. If Pareto[8] is to be believed you'll likely find 20% of your customers are responsible for 80% of your profit.

Let them know they are your best customers and thank them. People will be happy to know that you acknowledge them as their best customers and appreciate their business. Providing something extra for your best clients will bring more benefit to your company than the traditional end-of-year gift for all customers. (You might still want to give them that reminder each year.)

Tell them that they have extra benefits, that they haven't asked for.

There really is no downside.

---

[8] http://en.wikipedia.org/wiki/Pareto_principle

The number one thing you should do, and do it now

3: What business are you in?

One of the most important factors you need to define is exactly what business you are in. Here's a hint: it's unlikely to be "video production", "editing", "motion graphics", "DVD Authoring" or any similarly defining terms.

First and foremost you are in the business of making other people money. Yes, you are in business to make money yourself, but if that's your focus then you'll be less likely to succeed than an approach that puts the focus on making your clients money. How you apply your skills to that clear proposition is the business that you are in.

One of the reasons the railroads lost their influence and power – remember at one time anti-trust legislation was used against their actions – was that they thought they were in the railroad business, as one might think we are in the production or post-production business. The problem with the railroads was that there were other businesses that came to stomp on their near-monopoly of the *transport* business.

The railroad companies didn't see cars, trucks and aircraft as competition because the new transportation companies didn't run railroads. However, they were all in the transport business and customers were siphoned off to faster (aircraft) and more direct (trucks) or flexible (trucks) options than the fixed routes and large payloads necessary for rail to operate.

Don't make the same mistake. If you're in the business of shooting video, then anyone with a camera is a competitor. You're probably not in the business of editing video – even if that's all you do day in and day out! You're more likely to be in the business of making order out of chaos, or attempting to make sow's ears into less-ugly sow's ears, sometimes referred to as "polishing t*rds".

It's the talent, not the tools

Never fall into the trap of defining yourself by your tools – I'm talking to you 'Avid Editors'! When all the tools of our trades were expensive, the equipment used was a quick shortcut to defining quality. Someone who worked with Beta SP could deliver a "broadcast quality" product beyond the reach of someone with less expensive SVHS equipment.

Such self-definition became a liability when the tools of production dropped in price and former clients started buying gear. What you were really selling all along was what you could *do* with the equipment: the talent and story-telling ability. Those skills are not easily obtained nor easily reproduced. Even when equipment costs drop, your skills do not lose value.

Focus on the Unique Selling Proposition, not the marketplace

The most successful businesses do not try to be everything for everyone. I made that mistake early in my career. My first company, Charisma Video Productions, offered video production services "for everyone". Unfortunately, "for everyone" in a secondary city in 1980 wasn't all that many people.

Over time it became clear that I enjoyed, and therefore was good at, education and training video, particularly where I could do dramatic reenactments. Once I realized that was our niche, business started to grow. People knew what they should call us for. After 30+ weddings, I was happy to leave that as an opportunity for someone else!

Ultimately, your business is about making other people money. That's the only reason they come to you, because they perceive that your work will help them make more money than without you. You need to do everything to re-enforce that notion with your branding and marketing efforts.

When you're determining your unique proposition – the thing you do better than anyone else – look around at your competition. Chances are no-one is really trying to go after a smaller niche, leaving those opportunities clear for you to find one (or more) that you can excel at.

Never try to create a unique selling proposition that you cannot deliver on. If your unique selling proposition is that you support "every format", you'd better know how to work with EIA-J ½" on short notice! If you don't, people will be disappointed and, instead of your business coming to mind when they have a need that matches your unique selling proposition, they will avoid disappointment again, and go elsewhere, undoing all your marketing and advertising efforts.

Focusing your Unique Selling Proposition

Once you have identified where there are opportunities that match your capabilities, write it down. There's something about being forced to write ideas down that helps cement them. The goal is to reduce your unique selling proposition to one paragraph. It's no big deal if you start with 2-3 paragraphs. Ideally you'd be able to reduce it to a 'mantra[9]' – a simple 2-4 word summary of the way you make money for others.

Once you have a first draft, edit, edit and edit some more. Pare out the generalities and vague promises. Rework it until it's a lean, clear statement of the value (your brand promise, as we'll see) you bring to your customers.

The ultimate test of the clarity of the unique selling proposition is whether your non-industry receptionist understands it and can tell you what is your value to your customers. For the acid-test, run it past your non-industry family and see if it communicates to them.

Once you have a clear Unique Selling Proposition, you have a foundation for your brand, marketing, advertising and every interaction with your customers. You'll take every opportunity to get that unique selling proposition communicated to new and old customers alike.

---

[9] http://blog.guykawasaki.com/2006/01/mantras_versus_.html

4: Clarify your Brand

Your brand is your business' personality. It's the promise(s) you make to the world about your business. Branding defines who you are and what your business promises customers. Your marketing is how you express that in every interaction with the public or customers. Similarly, branding is not advertising. Advertising is how you raise awareness of your brand and marketing.

To put it another way:

> "Your product or service is not your company's brand and neither is your logo or your business card. Your brand is the genuine "personality" of your company."

> **"It's what your customers think of you and say about you when they're away from your company."**

> It's important for you to define your brand and what you stand for, because if you don't your customers won't have a clear grasp of who you are and what you stand for in business. The risk of not having a clearly defined brand is that someone else – media or competitor – will define it for you. In the absence of a clearly defined brand, that externally applied brand will likely become your story. It's unlikely to be telling your story the way you want it told, though.

In a Business Week article "A Practical Guide to Branding"[10] author Karen E. Klein said:

"First you create the brand, then you raise awareness of it"

Branding is the creation of your company's personality and promise. It happens before determining marketing or advertising, because without a clearly defined brand behind the marketing and advertising, the expenditure will be mostly wasted.

To some extent, your Brand is the founding point for all the stories you'll be telling in your marketing. As we'll learn later, marketing is essentially good storytelling and advertising is getting those stories heard. There are ways to get your story heard that don't require payment.

---

[10] http://www.businessweek.com/smallbiz/content/jun2008/ sb2008069_694225.htm

Developing your brand

Think about what you want the company's personality to be. If you're a small company or one controlled by one or two people, the personality of the company is likely to be similar to the owners.

Steve Celi, a copywriter and verbal-branding expert with Where Words in San Carlos, CA, says:

> "A brand is a promise and branding is the act of devising the promise your company makes to the world."

Your promise is, of course, your Unique Selling Proposition.

To develop your brand, gather your most trusted friends/executives/employees together and devise the promise that your company is going to make to the world. Some sample branding promises might be:

> "To delight the customer by providing more than they expect and everything they pay for."

> "To only provide work of the highest technical and creative quality, regardless of cost."

> "To cost-effectively build the visual communications tools that make our clients money."

In a world where production and post-production services are rapidly becoming a commodity, and we're increasingly competing with new entrants to the industry who are putting price pressure on the industry. Without a clearly defined brand customers will choose solely on the basis of price or because they can get something for free. If you've got a brand then you're selling a "lifestyle" and you can sell anything against that brand.

Most people will be familiar with Coca Cola – caffeinated sugary water in reality – but Coke's brand is that of the soda you have when you're young, attractive and having fun.

Make your world smaller

The Digital Production BuZZ was the best talk-radio show for Digital Production, Post Production and Distribution that combined cutting edge technologies, budget filmmaking with insightful analysis in a fun atmosphere. I can confidently make that claim because I defined the "world" that we able to be best within, very narrowly. As Seth Godin says[11] "The Secret to being the best in the world, is to make the 'world' smaller."

When you're thinking about your brand – promise and personality – define yourself as being the "best" at something:

> "The best place to online Final Cut Pro projects."

> "The best environment you've ever enjoyed for post production."

> "The best people in the best location."

> "The most highly technically skilled production company in Wilkes-Barre."

Whatever your focus, be the 'best' at something, even if it is a small world, after all.

When you make your world smaller you increase the chances of becoming an acknowledged leader in that smaller niche, rather than just another voice in a wider world.

Double your prices!

When people need to try harder to get work, most think of lowering their prices. Certainly that was my first thought during a period where we weren't returning as much on our capital investment in production gear as we should. After all, we were in a relatively small market even though it is the 6th largest in Australia, near the largest city in the country.

---

[11] http://sethgodin.typepad.com/seths_blog/2009/02/make-the-world-smaller.html

Being relatively new to business I hired a consultant. Most of the advice was very, very irrelevant to our business, with one exception. For the programs we'd independently produced (see "Own your content" later in this book) the consultant recommended doubling our pricing, after adding some training guides and exercises to the video programs we'd produced. We did just that and did not lose a single sale. We sold the same number of each program but made a lot more money, making the deal even sweeter.

Your price is part of your brand. Obviously, if your branding is Wal-mart (good enough quality at a dirt cheap prices) then doubling your price is not consistent with your brand. Conversely if you're focused on providing the highest quality, it's just as inconsistent with the brand to be the cheapest in your market. People associate quality with price and expect to pay more for quality.

Increasing your overall price structure has another benefit: people who pay more are nicer people. Budget focused customers (a.k.a. cheapskates) tend to want more and want to pay less. Clients focused on quality tend to expect to pay more and are nicer about it.

Seth Godin talks about the affect pricing has on your story in "Change your pricing[12]."

The American Express OPEN forum has an audio post called "Should You Lower Prices in a Downturn[13]?" with the summary:

> "Pricing and promotions are tricky to get right during recessions. Lower prices often guarantee only one thing — lower margins. And customers will expect those low prices to remain once the economy recovers. Otherwise, they'll be looking for new vendors. Yet doing nothing is almost certain to drive business away."

Certainly, holding price steady, or even increasing it, is a better strategy than dropping to the bottom of the barrel.

---

[12] http://sethgodin.typepad.com/seths_blog/2009/01/change-your-pri.html

[13] http://blogs.openforum.com/2008/12/17/audio-post-should-you-lower-prices-in-a-downturn/

Digital Production BuZZ

In 2005 I created an Internet talk-radio-style show called the
Digital Production BuZZ. The BuZZ was very different to the DV
Guys show I'd managed and co-hosted for four years. The
promises that formed the Digital Production BuZZ brand were:

- Honesty – no punches pulled

- Insight and perspective

- Professional (classic radio sense)

- Sometimes controversial

- Maybe a little blunt

- Great source for news and industry status

- Fun

I followed through on those promises by asking "hard" questions.
There's something quite satisfying seeing a PR representative for
a major NLE company turning even paler than she was, after my
(somewhat blunt) opening question for the guest she was
shepherding. But it was the question then on everyone's mind and
it wasn't being asked.

I feel confident that the brand we created was demonstrated
during the show, now part of Larry Jordan and Associates, with a
slightly different brand promise.

5:   Expand into new areas

Any period of less than full employment should be used to improve your skills, to expand your business or to create content you can own and get a return from long term.

Technology and techniques are evolving so fast that unless you are actively improving your skill base, you are falling behind. Optimally, regardless of workload, we all should be spending the equivalent of 20% of our workweek on improving our skills. Few, outside Google employees, can realistically find time to do that when our businesses are running hot, so we have to compensate by using any time when business is not running hot to improve our skills and improve our marketing.

Times of excess capacity are also an opportunity to expand your business. Keeping within the brand and Unique Selling Proposition you've worked on, how and where can you expand? Can you expand geographically into adjacent (or remote) locations? With the communication infrastructure of the Internet, you don't need to be local to fulfill your mission and be true to your brand.

It's also an opportunity to partner with complementary businesses to your mutual benefit.

Learn new skills

While you have the advantage of experience, those graduating from Film Schools, Universities and even Community Colleges have experience with Final Cut Pro, Media Composer, After Effects and usually a 3D application (like Cinema 4D or Maya). Photoshop skills are simply assumed: grade schoolers[14] are now doing visual effects and compositing!

Whatever new skills you learn, should be consistent with your brand and unique selling proposition. Most people's immediate thought is to broaden the range of services you offer, in the expectation of being able to satisfy more customer needs. Advance carefully, whether by improving your own skills or partnering with others, to keep true to your core brand values.

---

[14] http://www.boingboing.net/2009/03/10/terrific-special-eff.html

One of my friends, <u>Randy Tinfow</u>[15] of Image Plant and <u>Proscenum</u>, chose a different path. Instead of broadening their services, he chose to narrowly define their speciality. Randy says:

> "I have actually gone in the other direction, narrowly defining our perceived specialty or "value add" to be in an area of great demand. So by developing excellence in an area of need, we've been able to differentiate ourselves and have as much business as we can handle. We have not sold editing, animation, compression, or production in 5 years, but 80% of our activity is doing just those tasks. It's the other 20% of the work that pulls clients in our direction: "providing enhanced video delivery mechanisms."
>
> Being great in one important area is far better than being a good generalist. Certainly more lucrative. It helps that we can demonstrate how our works ALWAYS saves clients money."

By building one specific area of expertise – "enhanced video delivery mechanisms", including the entire <u>Proscenum</u>[16] delivery technology – Image Plant have grown their editing, animation, compression and production services without advertising or promoting them! You'll note the guarantee is that it "ALWAYS saves clients money".

Almost everyone will have to deal with non-tape workflows. These workflow changes are already upon us, so now is the time to read, and get test footage to become totally familiar with how to edit RED, XDCAM HD/EX, AVCHD/AVCCAM, etc., ahead of client needs. Or become an expert in getting media online with expertise in encoding and hosting. Inevitably it will drive production and post production.

---

[15] http://www.linkedin.com/pub/7/763/472

[16] http://www.proscenum.com/index.html

Expand into new areas

Resources

If you happen to be in Southern California then UCLA Extension in Hollywood offers everything from acting and animation to television writing and visual effects. Most courses at UCLA Extension and comparable schools meet for six to 12 weeks and cost a few hundred dollars. Longer, part-time certificate programs take up to two years to finish.

The various Guilds also have classes and resources for free through the Guilds' head offices. Lori Jane Coleman, American Cinema Editors internship director, encourages fellow editors who aren't on a show or film crew to take a Final Cut Pro class, which is offered free through the Guild.

Beyond these regional activities, companies like Lynda.com[17], Total Training[18] and Class on Demand[19] have both DVD-based training and online delivery of the same training.

> **Tip:** You'll get the most benefit out of any form of visual training by working along with the trainer, or immediately putting the skills into use with your own project materials. Passively watching online video or DVD rarely improves your knowledge. Actively applying what you've learnt within 24 hours cements it as knowledge in your brain. If you haven't used it within 72 hours (3 days) research shows that you wasted your time watching.

Don't forget that most software comes with tutorials. In the Final Cut Studio 2 package there are two DVDs of tutorial included free. You'll be surprised how many productivity tips can be learnt.

Studio Daily[20] and DV[21] run periodic webinars on relevant topics you can use to improve your skill base.

---

[17] http://www.lynda.com/

[18] http://www.totaltraining.com/

[19] http://www.classondemand.net/ClassOnDemand/index.aspx

[20] http://www.studiodaily.com/main/

[21] http://www.dv.com/

BuZZdex

One resource you should be using, wherever you are, is the Digital Production BuZZ BuZZdex[22]. The BuZZdex is an index to the best of free articles, tutorials and resources anywhere on the Internet. While we all know there are great tutorials at CreativeCow.net, throughout the Digital Media Net network and at places like LAFCPUG.org or KenStone.net, it is only through the BuZZdex that you can find articles from all these sites, and more, that are indexed by Application, Chapter and Topic.

For example, if you wanted to find an article on Chroma Keying DV in Final Cut Pro, you would go to the BuZZdex and choose "By Application." Select **Final Cut Pro** then **Articles & Tutorials by category**. Select **Keying** from the category list and the topic sublist will appear. From there you can choose **Keying DV** and three articles will be listed ready for your learning pleasure.

Or, if you wanted to know how to create a fake display on a monitor, choose **Articles** then **more Categories** under the **by Category** heading. Select **Visual and Creative Effects** as the chapter and **Simulating Displays**. Then simply choose the article that's closest to the type of display you want to create.

As of this writing (mid March 2009) the BuZZdex contained 7230 article or tutorial references to 4627 individual articles. (Some articles have more than one reference in the index because they fit under more than one topic.) No other resource comes even close. These can be further sorted into type, so if you only want to see video tutorials, you can limit the BuZZdex to only showing you video-based tutorials.

Expand Geographically

Back when I was living in Australia – in the dark ages of the 1990's – my business had to come from the local (6th largest city) market. Rarely would we get business from Sydney – just 60 miles away – looking to reduce costs on capital city pricing levels, but mostly it was local business. If there was no local business, we had "excess capacity" that we ultimately used to build a second income stream from self-produced content.

---

[22] http://www.digitalproductionbuzz.com/BuZZdex/

Now we can do business with clients removed from our local markets. Mainstream TV and Film production has been moving to global production for years. Movies and TV series are shot in Canada while postproduction is based in LA. There are whole businesses[23] dedicated to moving digital dailies from shoot location to editorial location as quickly as possible. Visual Effects are done where the expertise exists, be that Los Angeles, London, Wellington or Sydney. Projects I've been involved with have animation segments created and rendered in India for postproduction in Los Angeles.

Our first NAB in the US back in 2001, was before we knew local businesses, so we decided to continue using the same digital printer we'd had a long-term relationship with, based in Sydney. I uploaded the files from Los Angeles and they FedEx'd the printed materials to us in Las Vegas, direct to our hotel. (FedEx from Australia to the US was very cheap then as the volume went the opposite direction.)

My friend Rob Birnholz of Absolute Motion Graphics[24] lives in Florida but has clients across the USA, including one client he's been doing work for over the last three years, that he's never met face-to-face! Rob has built his business with strong word-of-mouth and his contributions to industry resources, like the International Media Users Group (IMUG) email group[25].

Before you get work remotely, you'll need to build a reputation and network of people who know you well enough to trust you to fulfill their needs, without micromanagement.

Day-to-day management of the process is by phone and web approval using QuickTime movies. One of Rob's clients, then based in Sleepy Hollow, NY, was in a client meeting and "called down" to the graphics department – i.e. Rob in Florida. Only when the client suggested it would be easier to just walk down to meet, was it necessary to reveal his true location.

_____

[23] http://www.signiant.com/

[24] http://amg.birnholz.com/

[25] http://www.imugonline.com/about/about.shtml

Top five steps to work remotely with clients

1. Build a solid reputation and network wherever you can. Rob presents at conferences and user group meetings to build his profile by sharing his knowledge generously.

2. Keep communication clear. Remote briefings require your best listening and communication skills. Feed back to the potential client what you believe their need to be, and follow up in written form – an email will do – so you're all on the same page as far as deliverables, schedule and creative content.

3. Share the work in progress regularly. Export, encode and upload work in progress so the client can see where it's going and how progress is being made.

4. Keep physical delivery schedules in mind. Whether you deliver by courier or upload, there will be significant time involved.

5. Use local talent for shoots at the client location. Many people in the IMUG group share information on location shoots and talent away from their base. Again networking will pay dividends for the time invested.

It's worth noting that Rob also uses remote access services to control his primary After Effects workstation while he is on the road.

Some other Tips

Submit your name to relevant website directories. Studio Daily has a jobs board[26], as does LAFCPUG.org[27] and some other user group sites.

Regularly review Mandy.com[28], which lists production jobs and services worldwide.

---

[26] http://jobs.studiodaily.com/c/search.cfm?site_id=1947

[27] http://www.lafcpug.org/phorum/list.php?2

[28] http://mandy.com/

Don't forget Craigslist.org[29] as they have classifieds for most major US cities with a TV/Film/Video category. Do a city by city search for work you're qualified to create, but only follow up on jobs offering to pay something you can afford to work for! (Ads on Craigslist often offer minimal, or no, pay and are not really for working professionals.)

Participate in forums and blogs sharing helpful advice and experience. Do NOT participate only to promote. You will fail and be perceived as a spammer. Participate and build your reputation and privately contact people who you think you can help.

Your blog, as we'll see, is a great place to advertise your expertise, by sharing. It's also a place for people to get a feel for your competence, personality and professionalism on their own time. Use it.

Partner with other business or add services

The classic local partner for a video production or postproduction business is an Advertising Agency. In a world where advertising budgets are shrinking, often dramatically, that's not necessarily going to be the most productive partner.

A far more logical partner in the age of rapidly growing web video, would be website designers. Specifically, target professional website designers looking to add video services to their customers' sites. You can be particularly valuable to them if you bring the whole production and encode skillset to the table. (If you are primarily a web design company, consider adding video encoding and hosting skills and partnering with local video producers to add your services to theirs.)

Network

The single most important thing you can do to build your local (and non-local) business is to network. If you have an MCA-I chapter nearby, join it and participate. Join the local small business council or even Rotary/Kiwanis/Lions club. Attend events. Get on the committee. If you need to build your business you have time to contribute.

---

[29] http://craigslist.org/

You will find compatible business this way. Once established within the group you'll find businesses that need your services

Create co-operative partnerships

The most common "relationship" between businesses is a simple agreement to use each other where the opportunity arises. Very few will need to go beyond that basic agreement.

Spend time getting to know the partner. Know their capabilities, view their work and generally get to know them. In the early phases, spend time over a meal or drinks to find out how compatible your values are. Values – standards of work, ways to treat clients, etc. – are important. Successful business relationships, like personal ones, will have compatible business values.

- "Always treat others as you would be treated." It's been a golden rule for a very long time but it remains good advice.

- Treat your business partners well. Together you can grow successfully.

- Pay bills on time.

- Communicate clearly and if there is any miscommunication, use soft negotiating skills to solve the problem without damaging the relationship. The Negotiation Guru30 has tips if you need advice.

- Keep plenty of business cards with you and give them away freely. Leave a supply at your partners' locations.

---

[30] http://www.thenegotiationguru.com/

Expand into new areas

6: Marketing, PR and Social conversations

Marketing is storytelling. People tell stories in conversations. Social Media/Social networking is about conversations: conversations with media, influencers, customers and the wider world. Here's how Stow Boyd defines[31] social media:

> "Social Media are those forms of publishing that are based on a dynamic interaction, a conversation, between the author and active readers, in contrast with traditional broadcast media where the 'audience' is a passive 'consumer' of 'content'. The annotations or social gestures left behind by active readers, such as comments, tags, bookmarks, and trackbacks, create an elaborate topology resting on the foundational blog posts, and this enhanced meta-environment, the blogosphere, is the context for and the realization of a global collaboration to make sense of the world and our place in it."

Before you start moving into social media-based marketing and communication, you need to understand the "story" you're telling with your company – this is your brand. The brand – the values, specialities and ways of doing business (i.e. your business' personality) – is not the same as the stories you create at your company. You'll want many of these stories, so that you have something relevant to each outlet that still brings people back to the central story of your company.

Marketing wizard Seth Godin explained in an article on The Difference between PR and publicity [32]:

> *"PR is the strategic crafting of your story. It's the focused examination of your interactions and tactics and products and pricing that, when combined, determine what and how people talk about you."*

---

[31] http://www.stoweboyd.com/message/2009/04/social-media-defined.html

[32] http://sethgodin.typepad.com/seths_blog/2009/03/the-difference-between-pr-and-publicity.html

For example, are you promising to create great video, change their life forever, or educate them? That's part of the story. How the company came into being is part of the story, and all that stuff you'll be blogging about is part of the story. Mr. Godin would remind you that a Purple Cow [33] is remarkable and the secret to publicity is to be remarkable!

The stories can be very subjective, but remember, each media outlet or blogger is only interested in certain types of stories. Most importantly the story must be interesting to other people. You might have heard this referred to as the "hook" – what makes a story interesting to a particular media outlet or blogger. Please don't pitch your story to irrelevant blog or media outlets. As someone who's been on the other end of that equation with the Digital Production BuZZ, it does you no favors to pitch to outlets that would never cover your story.

New PR is being part of the conversation.

To talk about "new PR" implies some difference from "old PR", or PR as it has been known. Traditionally PR – Public Relations – was something that was only really active when the company had a new product, version or customer – when something the company thought was newsworthy happened. Such news was distributed to the media by way of a "PR Consultant" who used their influence and relationship with members of the media to get the story printed. Most communication went out in a scattergun "Press Release" for mostly print media.

There was certainly no discussion of company strategy, internal debate, controversy or bad news. When these got mentioned, the traditional approach was to deny everything!

Done right (and it rarely is) traditional PR can be valuable to a small business. If you can afford it, a good PR consultant will:

- Target the appropriate outlets;
- Pitch the writer, who they have a personal relationship with, to get the story written;
- Organize background interviews; and

---

[33] http://www.amazon.com/gp/product/159184021X

• Follow up after the story runs.

Fundamentally Public Relations is about getting your company, products and brand known to the wider world. It is part of the effort that includes marketing and advertising. Many companies, particularly smaller companies, are finding that they get better results investing in PR 2.0 than from traditional PR and advertising combined.

This new approach to PR, like most of the modern social web, is more like a conversation. It is characterized by being more open and transparent to the whole company, a philosophy that goes back to the original Cluetrain Manifesto[34] from 1999. Markets are conversations, and PR is the conversations and stories you tell about your company.

It's very hard to separate your new PR efforts from the company blog, social media activities and building your network as they're all part of being part of the conversation, being part of the New Now.

Marketing is storytelling

Big event advertising – such as we see at the SuperBowl every year – is fun to do but rarely successful and certainly out of the price range for any production or postproduction business. That people are immune to advertising is tenet 74 of 1999's Cluetrain Manifesto about open and transparent communication with companies.

People are interested in genuine stories, so find your company's story and keep telling it, and always make it interesting. Don't be shy – every company, every individual, has a story and that story is your marketing. You're going to use that story to build up a tribe, because modern marketing isn't so much about advertising, but building a tribe of people who "follow" what you do for whatever reason.

---

[34] http://www.cluetrain.com/

Parental lessons

I only recently realized how important story is in marketing, and why my parents had been so successful in their various businesses. It comes right down to the fact that my mom loves to tell stories. There was always a story around any big promotion – it was my dad's birthday, or he wanted to do "this thing" (which involved all the dealers working harder and selling more) for my mom. Whatever they were doing in that business had a story associated with it and they were very successful Tupperware distributors as a result.

Years later, after retiring from that business, my mom started another – Gourmet (English-style boiled) Christmas Puddings. There was the whole story of my mother's Great, Great Grandmother's recipe; of all being hand made, boiled in a cloth; the story of how my mom first started this business for her Church out of gratitude to God for her brother's safe return from a tour of duty in Vietnam.

While managing that business, I was very careful to keep the image in line with that story: this was a "little old lady" hand making puddings in a family business. Every piece of communication was professional but not "slick." It all had to feel like it was just my mom and a few friends.

Later, when we were expanding the business to find year-round products, I created new fruit combinations using the same production process and surrounded them with "story" about how early settlers to Australia couldn't find their traditional fruits so they experimented with local fruits instead. (I know this story was the true original story, because I made it up!)

When it came time to create a very traditional coin-in-pudding we researched the story of why people put a coin in the pudding because we wanted to tell that story with the product. No-one seemed to know the history but was sure their "grandmother would have known." It turns out the history wasn't that appealing (the "lucky" person who got the token was the sacrifice so the rest of the village – those who got to live – would do well) so we created a more palatable "story" around the tradition that better fit with the common perception that the coin was indicative of a good year ahead for the person who found it.

Application to production and postproduction

I believe it's genuinely hard to promote a production and post-production business through traditional advertising. Yellow pages advertising didn't work for my Australian production business. I think most of us rely on networking and word-of-mouth, but I always felt there was an opportunity to promote what we could do to local businesses that may never consider video production, or were simply unaware.

I discovered this fun kids toy that was a small plastic rubbery animal with a low-stick adhesive. These were designed to be thrown at walls and to slowly creep their way down the wall. They were inexpensive at less than $5 each. As I read a business success story in the local newspapers – particularly the mid-week freebie – I would send these business owners one of the toys with the message: "Congratulations on your recent (named) success. Things are obviously going well for you at the moment and that's great. When you strike those moments of frustrations, relieve the tension by throwing this toy at the wall. If your frustration is about video production, call us."

The story was simple: "We're involved in our community – because we noticed what was happening – and we're here to help with any video need."

Now, I can't quantify the success of the approach – mostly because our business took a major change in direction about six months into what I considered would be a multi-year effort – but I did hear back that we made an impression on people, and they'd kept the toy around (keeping around a reminder of our company).

Preparing your story

There's no point in approaching any writer – journalist or blogger – about your project until you're prepared. As Mr. Godin said "be remarkable." Craft an interesting story(s) that readers, listeners or viewers will be interested in. Don't think that your story will appeal to "everyone." It won't and the better you understand who your customer is, the easier it will be to find writers who will think their audiences will be interested in your remarkable company.

> "If your company does not have a 'remarkable' story, then that's your first challenge – find or create one. Be a purple cow."

Keep the story simple. If I have a problem when writing my marketing stories, it's making them too complicated. Of course, our software products do so much it's hard to simplify. I should have learnt from my mother and father whose stories were always simple and straightforward. As I now realize from her blog posts, my mother is a terrific storyteller – no wonder she was good at marketing. (See, even my 79 year old mother has a blog – why don't you?)

Which story is more interesting: "A great new software tool" or "The scariest tool you'll ever see"? Along with that gem – that consistently appeared when Michael Horton wrote anything about The Assistant Editor[35] – Michael also encouraged me to "tell a story" in the original presentation.

So when we announced the product, it was in the context of a "true story" about an editor many weeks into a project who'd finished logging but couldn't get started. Enter "The Assistant Editor" (later launched as First Cuts). The story made it easier for people to understand the value, and it made it easier to structure a presentation because it was just the story.

A simple story: "When you're up against impossible deadlines then First Cuts can make it possible to meet the deadline in ways never before available."

Seems like yet another time when listening to my mother was a good idea!

In simplifying your stories keep in mind Guy Kawasaki's Mantras versus Mission[36]. He's talking about replacing boring corporate mission statements with simple mantras, aiming for a three-word summary of the essence of what you're about. Keep both in mind when you're preparing the pitch.

To get a clearer idea of how your story might be of interest to others, ask yourself these questions:

What makes your company interesting?

What is remarkable?

What have we done that no-one has ever done before?

---

[35] http://www.assistedediting.com/FirstCuts/

[36] http://blog.guykawasaki.com/2006/01/mantras_versus_.html

Frankly, if you can't discover how your company is unique/ interesting/exciting then perhaps it isn't and you should reconsider, or plan on spending many thousands of dollars communicating an uninteresting story with advertising. Or focus on user stories as do many AJA print advertisements in trade magazines.

Consider these examples for inspiration. The company might be "the first to use xyz technology" (the first company to shoot with RED in your area for example) or a project you're working on is remarkable. I managed to be remarkable in 1994 in Newcastle by being the first postproduction company to adopt any Non Linear Editing software (Media 100). This was remarkable enough at the time to get quite a bit of press coverage.

If you add Flash skills to your company's skill set, talk about how effective rich media is. (You'll need to do some research but that's part of the effort.)

Your company may have a particular approach, might work in a consistently interesting area, or be filling a need no-one else can. If I'd been more aware at the time of how valuable remarkable stories are, I would have promoted the series of training packages we created by telling the story of how it came to be and how we, a local company, were filling a national need that no-one else was prepared to fill. A project you're working on may have been completed in an unusual location; or have an unusual workflow.

Build your people as experts on more than just the company

You can build a story around the people in your company. What famous productions they've worked on, who they've worked with, etc. These kind of stories may make good material for your website and blog but they probably won't get you coverage in any media.

All media – journalists, bloggers – need expert sources. Few journalists have any background in production so build yourself, and your employees where appropriate, as an expert they can refer to.

If there's a local story on anything related to video, high definition, or broadcast television you want the reporters to know where they have a local expert. A local expert who will get their name and company affiliation attached to the story when it runs – as an expert!

Build some interesting presentations about the business and your experience of it. Rehearse these and then offer to be guest speaker at your local Rotary, Kiwani or other service organization. Many church groups are also regularly looking for speakers. The more presentations that you make, the more credible you are as an expert on your subject matter.

Take every opportunity to help a reporter, even if it doesn't directly benefit your company in the short term. Be sure to talk about your competition in complimentary terms if it's being discussed. You're being interviewed because you are an expert, not because you speak for your company (in this case).

Get on the mailing list for Peter Shankman's "Help a Reporter Out[37]" (HARO) daily mailings. Two or three times a day he sends out an email that lists a range of topics that reporters around the country are looking for people to interview about.

For the last three years, we – as a company – have been concentrating on differentiating Intelligent Assistance from the pack by having its CEO – that would be me – talk on "bigger picture" subjects, leaving the Final Cut Pro specific subjects for other equally competent presenters. So in that time I've become a minor expert on trends in postproduction business and technology and an expert in digital distribution. These just happen to be the subjects I cover and part of the title of my blog as well.

Be human

The Cluetrain Manifesto[38] I mentioned at the start of this chapter, should be the next thing you read. It contains 95 theses, the first six of which are:

1. Markets are conversations.

2. Markets consist of human beings, not demographic sectors.

---

[37] http://www.helpareporter.com/

[38] http://www.cluetrain.com/

3. Conversations among human beings *sound* human. They are conducted in a human voice.

4. Whether delivering information, opinions, perspectives, dissenting arguments or humorous asides, the human voice is typically open, natural, uncontrived.

5. People recognize each other as such from the sound of this voice.

6. The Internet is enabling conversations among human beings that were simply not possible in the era of mass media.

Traditional PR tended to put a positive spin on everything the company did – not that there's anything wrong with that – but we all now recognize "PR speak" as being something different from the language we use in normal human conversation.

In the modern era – the New Now – people value genuine conversations, over PR speak and verbiage that is frequently likened to male cow dung.

There will be open and honest conversation around your company, and you can participate in it or have it happen without your story being heard. You are better off being part of the conversation about your company as an equal, not as 'the authority'. I'll be discussing how to monitor the conversations about your company later in this section.

Dealing with Bad News

When things are not going well, the last thing customers and other interested parties want to hear is obfuscation and partial truth. Unless you're Apple (and you are not) then a simple, open, truthful voice is what people want to hear.

If you have good news, tell the world how it will make their life better, if you have bad news, tell everyone why it happened, what you're going to do about it, and how you'll prevent it happening in the future.

While transparency will mostly be seen in your dealings with the media and in your blog, it should pervade every part of the company – whether that company is just you, or you and 200 of your closest work associates.

Think like a the media outlet

Please take this one to heart because you don't want to end up in the Bad Pitch Blog[39]. During the time I was editing a news feed for the Digital Production BuZZ I was inundated with thousands of press releases that were totally irrelevant to digital production, postproduction and distribution – my beat. Clearly many PR people do not filter their story to the outlet, instead blasting everyone possible. A simple, quick visit to the feed's website would have made it very obvious that "Voice over IP" topics were not relevant!

Think like the media outlet. It should be obvious but if you don't you're not only wasting the effort expended in sending out the story to that outlet, but you're sending a clear message to the reporter that you don't care about their time, and are happy to waste it.

Before sending out an announcement, know who you're sending it to. Read their previous stories and know what they cover. If they're a blogger be already known to them by having read and commented on their blog as an interested reader.

To my surprise, when I went to *The Conversation* conference in late 2008, I was already known to one of the conference organizers because I had posted comments on their blog.

So consider carefully where you want to release your information. Know the reporter and the outlet and *think like them*. Put on their filters and send them information that's relevant to their beat – the area that they cover.

When you do send a release, make sure the subject line and the first couple of lines of the email explain exactly why it's of importance to the journalist's audience. You'll have at most 15-20 seconds to make your point before the recipient hits delete!

---

[39] http://badpitch.blogspot.com/

Find the communities who would be interested in your pitch

News outlets meet the needs of their advertisers and readers or viewers. So, along with vetting which outlets you should be working with look also for other communities that would be interested in your information.

If you favor educational production, find local and online outlets that target those communities and send your releases and information to those outlets.

If your expertise is in trade show video or company promotion, find out who else has complementary businesses with communities attached that you can connect with.

Use the right medium for the story

Local news outlets are rarely the right medium for a postproduction, production or distribution success story. Or any story on the subject. Maybe if they have a "tech" section, but generally speaking, the people you want to reach won't be reading the tech section in the weekly "Star" (or whatever the local newspaper is called). Local TV might be open to running a story but again, is that where your potential customer is?

I remember reading – so far back I can't attribute it – that giant sports promoter IMG was trying to convince the CEO of IBM to advertise at a major golf tournament. Mr CEO says "why would we advertise at a golf event? The only people who attend are executives like myself... Oh, I see your point." The best venue for your story is one where the people you want to reach – potential and existing customers – are already engaged.

Targeting a different outlet may mean targeting a different form of media. Podcasts require audio content (generally by interview), or video and audio content. Whatever the outlet, tailor the content and media to that outlet. Be flexible – it's about them and their audience, not about you.

The pitch letter

You would never send out a press release or other pitch to a blogger or journalist without a cover letter. That cover letter, as I mentioned earlier, gives you 15-20 seconds – tops – to convince the writer that this story would be interesting to their audience.

A pitch letter that strikes the right note lets the writer know that you understand your own business and how it fits into their beat or interest. The first thing that will happen is that the writer will be shocked that you actually researched the outlet before making the pitch. In my Digital Production BuZZ days, those who did pitch the story perfectly at my audience were all ultimately interviewed on the show, because I did have to find guests! I loved getting pitches like those because it made my life easier and helped me program the show.

Conversely the majority of pitches never got beyond a cursory read of the subject line and first paragraph. Pitches were deleted in 4-5 seconds! So that subject line and first paragraph are incredibly important.

Don't tell the whole story with the pitch – that is the substance of the story after all – but enough to pique someone's interest for more on the story. You'll go with the hook and hope the writer bites down on the tasty morsel in the pitch!

So here are the top five tips to help compose pitch letters that work from the Bad Pitch Blog[40], as adapted by me for production folk.

Hit it with your best shot

Make that first sentence jump out and grab their interest. You're looking for a response like "I never knew"; "Wow, that's interesting"; or "That's a whole new angle to a story we're already covering."

Use no buzzwords, industry jargon or unnecessary hype. Hype ("revolutionary", "fantastic" etc.) will likely get your pitch caught in the spam trap.

---

[40] http://badpitch.blogspot.com/2009/02/five-crucial-tips-for-perfect-pitch.html

Make it personal

The pitch should be written directly for the recipient. Sure most of the talking points that make up the bulk of the pitch will be similar across all your pitches, but the first sentence *must* specifically for that recipient, targeted to their interest.

That way you'll get the 15-20 second view not the 5-second delete!

Address the letter to the writer using their name. Spell their name correctly.

Customize the pitch to the method

If you're sending something by physical mail, instead of email, which is what I've been talking about up until now, you'll need to tailor the pitch to the medium.

If you're sending hard copy, ONLY send it by messenger or FedEx/UPS. These get ignored much less often than regular postal service mail. I disagree with the Bad Pitch Blog about sending a fax. Faxes are most easily ignored – even if people have access to them in the New Now!

In a hard letter you can add more information, and probably a teaser message on the envelope to get it opened.

Write carefully and thoughtfully

The whole process of finding the right targets and reviewing their work and interest area and writing the pitch takes time. Do each step carefully and thoughtfully.

Proofread, and have someone else proofread

Print the letter to proofread it. Read it out loud. Have someone else read it. Do whatever you have to do to make sure there are no typographical or grammatical errors. Do not assume that passing a spell check gives you an error-free letter.

An additional set of eyes, preferably previously unrelated to the project, will give you fresh insight into the pitch and be another chance to catch errors.

Don't send PDFs

Now: a bonus tip from me! I know you want to present your pitch and story with perfect layout and design but make the pitch letter, if an email, short and at the top of the email. By all means attach a Rich Text (RTF) version so the writer can copy quotes from your story. MS Word will export RTF. Most people can read MS Word .doc formats but support for the more modern .docx format is not universal.

Avoid making your story unreadable after the writer has become interested. PDF documents are hard to copy from and the last thing you want to do is make it hard for the writer to tell your story to their audience.

I prefer to see the text, or at least a summary of the story, inside the email, following the pitch. Whether you attach a RTF or Word document, and/or include the text inside the email, do not even think about sending a PDF.

Be and know Influencers

Influential people are influential for two reasons: either they hold a position of power by writing for a major media outlet (print, radio, television or online); or they have credibility among their peers. People trust them for having honest, unbiased, and deep, information.

So, you get to become an influencer by having deep knowledge and an honest opinion you're prepared to share. (Or you could get employed at a media outlet, but that would conflict with your production business!) This influence is very easy to lose.

In some circles I'm considered an influencer: I have decent knowledge and am never short of an honest opinion. I strive to be unbiased in recommendation if not in personal choice. However, I had to threaten to sue someone who accused me of "being in the pocket" of a company who's product I rated highly and he did not. Apparently he believed that only those people paid off by the company would have a different opinion than his. I had to threaten to sue – going as far as having an attorney write a first demand for withdrawal of the comment – before he did finally withdraw it, because the accusation potentially damaged my reputation of impartiality.

As someone who, at the time, wrote reviews and interviewed people on DV Guys and (later) the Digital Production BuZZ, my objectivity was what made my opinion valuable. I had to fight to maintain that, as does every influencer. Influence is easily lost if betrayed.

That is why it's hard to turn an influencer on to your company (or product) without it ever appearing that they have become a shill for any organization.

The influencers most valuable to your production or postproduction business in the New Now are probably not those that work in local media. Obviously that coverage can be valuable, but more likely, the influencers you need to reach are at Rotary, Church, Kiwanis or Lions Club.

First Ten

Seth Godin talks about the "First Ten[41]"

> "This, in two words, is the secret of the new marketing.
>
> Find ten people. Ten people who trust you/respect you/ need you/listen to you...
>
> Those ten people need what you have to sell, or want it. And if they love it, you win. If they love it, they'll each find you ten more people (or a hundred or a thousand or, perhaps, just three). Repeat."

The 'new marketing' is word of mouth. These first ten are to become your evangelists and influencers. I'll be discussing creating evangelists a little bit later, but the first ten you need to find to promote your production or postproduction business are the influencers who'll get on board with the value you bring to your customers.

---

[41] http://sethgodin.typepad.com/seths_blog/2009/04/first-ten-.html

Find Influencers

Who are the influencers? They're all around you but probably not who you think they are. Before you go looking for influencers, you should have a very clear idea who your ideal and potential customers are. (No point going *looking* for less-than-ideal customers. They'll come along as well so we should focus on the ideal customer.)

Look for the pain

What are the pain points your customers (or potential customers) are feeling? What are the pain points in *their* business that *your* business solves?

Once you know what and where the pain points are for your customers, you can determine where they currently seek resolution of the pain – their current solution(s) to their business communication needs.

The people that are already alleviating the pain of your potential customers are a likely to be influencers. Build relationships with those people.

Run a blog search

Use Google Blog Search[42] for keywords that you're using for SEO on your website, and see which blogs come up consistently. You might also try a wider search for the keywords, but blogs will give better answers for online influencers. Add local criteria if you only want to work locally.

Find the top ten and follow their blog. Comment on the blog and, when you have something to contribute, contact them personally with your story.

> **Tip:** Regularly ask your customers what they would likely search for to find your business if they didn't know you. The answers can be very helpful in determining keywords.

Who writes about your industry

A great way to identify key influencers is to take a look at who writes about products and services in your industry. Start with the

---

[42] http://blogsearch.google.com/

local media and analysts who are covering your competition and see who they connect with.

In your Network

Being part of your local business community is one of the most valuable ways to find influencers. Since most production and postproduction customers are a business of one sort or another, except for event videography, when your influencers are the event organizers, clergy and caterers.

You'll find influencers among people in your local and extended business network.

Ask

While it's the obvious answer, few people bother to ask their customers who may have influenced them to do business with you. Not only will you find out who are the influencers, but you'll probably get useful feedback on how people hear about your business, and why they made the decision to do business with you.

Build your own community and turn your community into your influencers

Build your own community, using the ideas coming up in the networking segment, and become the influencer. You may be able to build a community around your company, but most people more easily build a community around a personality. People like people.

Provide your best customers with information, inside tips and special service and let them become your advocates. Word of mouth is the most valuable networking/influencing effect we can take advantage of.

Keep in mind the Cluetrain Manifesto when entering into these types of community communication: be open, honest and transparent. You represent your company at all times.

High-performance workstation company BOXX enlists leading digital artists, film compositors, film editors who use their workstations as advocates for their unique hardware. By picking those on the cutting edge of their industry, these customer advocates help BOXX create the impression that they're the "cool underdog" to Dell and HP!

These influencers would, ideally, form the foundation of your evangelists. Get an influencer interested in your company and you'll gain a lot more exposure and credibility than placing thousands of dollars worth of advertising in traditional media. You don't want to reach everyone, just those who are likely to need the services and benefits you can offer.

Another great way to find influencers is to network extensively.

Network

Production has always been a network-based business, except we didn't say it like that until the New Now. Back then it was "it's not what you know, it's who you know"! Same thing: knowing a lot of people is what networking is about. One expert suggests that 70% of media positions are filled from within someone's 'social' network.

There are two types of networks in the New Now: face-to-face local networks such as the MCA-I, Lions, Rotary, Kiwanis, Shriners, etc; and the online, 'social media' world of LinkedIn, Facebook and MySpace.

Get involved in your industry

If there is a local chapter of the Media Communication Association – International[43] (MCA-I), join it. You should also consider joining the Digital Video Professionals Association[44] (DVPA) for online resources.

If you're more focused on Event Videography, the Association of Video Professionals[45], or the Wedding and Event Videography Association International[46] might be more appropriate.

Don't just join and do nothing. The people who benefit most from any industry organization are those who contribute. Yes, it is extra work but volunteer for the committee. Help organize programs, make announcements and generally get yourself known as a helpful, knowledgeable professional.

---

[43] http://www.mca-i.org/

[44] http://www.dvpa.com/

[45] http://www.aovpros.com/

[46] http://www.weva.com/

Beyond local organizations, get involved with issues that will affect the industry. Know when there are tax changes that would adversely affect your business. Know when regulation is going to get in the way or other important issue. Right now, people are concerned about shifts in frequency allocation and the reduction of bands suitable for radio microphones that could lead to increased interference. If you use radio mics, be involved.

Get involved in your local business groups.

Whatever local business groups there are in your area, you should be in at least one and be involved. You will meet other business people, be introduced to the movers and shakers in the town (a.k.a. influencers)

Social Media

Social media is the phenomena of connecting online with business people and old friends/acquaintances. It includes social networking sites like LinkedIn for business networks, or Facebook and MySpace for personal networks. While there are other social networks, like Plaxo, these three are the primary social and business networks you need to belong to.

Social media is also used to describe any online site or tool that allows users to interact with other users and visitors. So, if you can leave a comment on a post, vote on content or rearrange the design of a site, then it is 'social media.'

According to Business Week online[47], the main reason small business should be using social media is because it's free:

> "The biggest reason to use social media is that it's free. You can be a significant player online without laying out any cash, and in this economic environment cash is king more than ever. It does take time, though, and in business time is money. But getting up to speed on social media is like learning to ride a bike; it's difficult and intimidating at first, but once you get the hang of it you can get where you want to go quickly—and even enjoy the ride."

---

[47] http://www.businessweek.com/smallbiz/content/jan2009/ sb20090116_666697.htm

Facebook

As well as your personal profile on Facebook you should also create a fan group for your company. On Facebook, I'm in groups formed to promote the Final Cut Pro Network and Supermeets; the Boston Final Cut Pro User Group, LA Mixers (Internet Technology and Multimedia); and Goodnight Burbank.

Brett Gaylor used Facebook to promote his documentary, *RiP: A Remix Manifesto*[48]. They create Facebook events you can 'attend' for each of the film's screenings. They also created an RSS feed that lets you know about the film; created a Twitter channel and had the traditional "keep me posted" box for email addresses.

MySpace

While the momentum seems to be moving away from MySpace toward Facebook, if you can dedicate the time to maintaining two communities there's no reason not to also have a production presence on MySpace.

LinkedIn

LinkedIn is more a service for business connections, so you'll want to be there and connect to anyone who could help promote your company or who is associated with it in any way (like customers). It is also very successful at promoting yourself. I have been approached with job offers because of my LinkedIn profile.

Here are some tips to better use LinkedIn to help grow your business:

1. You should link to your public LinkedIn profile in your email signature line.

   Change the URL for your public profile at LinkedIn so that it better represents your name. The default for my profile was some combination of numbers and letters that made no sense.

   Log into your Profile and go to the "Edit Profile" section. At the bottom of your profile is the link to your public profile and a button to edit it. My public profile is now available at http://www.linkedin.com/in/philiphodgetts, which is much

---

[48] http://www3.nfb.ca/webextension/rip-a-remix-manifesto/

easier to remember or share. I could have used a product or company name as well. Your custom URL must contain 5 – 30 alphanumeric characters without spaces, symbols, or special characters.

Write reviews and recommendations for different people across different industries or cultures. Spread your name into as many places as possible.

2. Put as much detail as possible into your profile. Keep going until it's 100% complete according to LinkedIn. Filling in the whole profile lets people know you treat it seriously and so should they.

3. Join LinkedIn groups that make sense for you and your business. I'm currently a member of the Boston Final Cut Pro User group, Digital Media LA (dmla), FCPUG Network Community and Supermeet, Inside Digital Design Radio and TV, Marketing – Video connect, Television Editors Avid and Final Cut Pro, and VOD Connect.

4. Only ask for connections from those you have some real association with. I'll happily connect with anyone I know in person, online or have met at a conference.

5. Update your status every couple of days because it shows you're involved and active on the site. I give this advice but do not always update that regularly!

6. Be optimistic and pleasant in anything you write. Being pleasant gets you noticed.

Many thanks to my friend Dean Forss[49] for suggesting most of these tips on how to get more out of LinkedIn. Most would apply to other social networks as well. For more information on using LinkedIn for business can be found in the regular postings of the "I'm on Linked In, now what???"[50] blog.

---

[49] http://www.linkedin.com/in/deanforss

[50] http://imonlinkedinnowwhat.com/

Be part of the conversation

Good conversations are dialogs. If you've been reading linearly through this book, you'll have realized that part of the New Now is the way conversations have moved online and across territory. Being part of the conversation is important. It keeps your name out there, and by extension your business name if you include it in your signature lines.

My primary take-away from the Cluetrain Manifesto is the importance of open communication with customers and clients in a natural, human voice instead of some PR-speak or corporate-speak, which comes across as terribly fake.

Being part of the conversation requires knowing where it's going on. The first starting point is a company blog (see the next section) with comments left open. Moderating comments, beyond killing spam, is one place where it can all go horribly wrong. Avoid anything that could be interpreted as censorship.

I recently commented on the blog post of an Internet provider who had some significant outages. The explanation was thorough but I felt the need to offer some quite negative feedback about the outage and the reasons behind it. Basically they were a year behind telling people what was going on and what they were doing about it hoping to avoid the service outage that occurred.

My post was held for moderation. That's fair because spam is a problem. (Posts on my personal blog at philiphodgetts.com are moderated for a first-time poster only. Subsequent posts from that person are immediately posted. Some spam does slip through Akismet.)

However, 3 hours later dozens of other, mostly very positive, posts were cleared and yet mine, being negative, was not. This was on a blog post about how open the company was, and a company that has openness in its service guarantee!

By the time 6 hours had gone past, and I finally received a call from the VP of business development, I had already drafted a rather scathing post for my own blog. Not about the outage problem, but about the fact that the company touted openness, when it practiced censorship of negative posts. It is fair to note that this company has now implemented a 'transparency initiative' to improve their communication and transparency and that the VP of business development did not consider what had happened to be acceptable.

Censorship will always come back to hurt you much more than any post. Negative posts about our companies are never fun or enjoyable, but they are valuable, because they show where we can improve, even if the improvement is one of communication.

Tracking Buzz

The big wide world of the web is vast, but conversations about you and your company can be tracked in nearly real-time, wherever they're posted.

You'll want to listen to conversations about your name and company name, your product names, your competition and Intelligent Assistance. OK, you don't have to watch my company but if you do, you'll find I respond quickly.

People are surprised that I even notice they've commented about something I'm interested in. This was particularly valuable post-NAB 2008 as I looked for any reference to our NAB announcement of "The Assistant Editor." By following blog postings I was able to organize participation in an online talk show, giving us even more coverage.

Set up blog searches

In order to be part of the conversations about your business, you should set up watchers at both blogsearch.google.com and technorati.com. What these two services do is monitor the conversations in the blogosphere and send you alerts, via an RSS feed, whenever your specific keywords are mentioned. I have searches at both that monitor product names, my own name and our companies' names.

You will get many "false positives" if your business name contains multiple words. Google's blogsearch feature in particular will trigger if *any* of the words match. There doesn't seem to be any way to force it to match all words in "Open TV Network", for example.

Even with so many false positives these are great tools for knowing who's talking about your business, what they're saying and where they're saying it. When you see your business discussed, join in the conversation where it's happening.

Search other social media

While I do not use either of these services – mostly because I don't Twitter, at least not yet – they do come recommended[51] by my friend Andrew Warner at Mixergy and I'm happy to pass them along.

"Twitter's Advanced Search – Use this tool to hear what people say on Twitter. It works really well on a mobile phone, so you can stay on top of conversations from anywhere."

"Backtype – This service will let you keep up with what's being said in blog comments. In the demo video included with the post on Mixergy.com, you can see how it might save your company's reputation."

There are other tools for tracking social media comments at Master New Media[52].

Lead a Tribe

Obviously you and your employees are going to be evangelists for your company, but to really build a bigger business you need to attract people who are otherwise not connected to the business to be evangelists and spread the word. This is a low budget alternative to spending more on advertising and promotion than you did setting up your facility.

The Tribe will be formed regardless of your involvement if your company is at all interesting. Your role is to make it easy for that tribe to form and communicate. A tribe cannot exist without the ability for the tribe members to communicate with each other. This is why the social media tools – forums, email newsletters and Facebook groups are so valuable. They enable members of your evangelist tribe to communicate with each other.

As Seth Godin (the high priest of tribe management) says[53]:

---

[51] http://blog.mixergy.com/eavesdrop-tools/

[52] http://www.masternewmedia.org/buzz-tracking-social-media-monitoring-best-tools-to-do-ego-searching-mini-guide/

[53] http://sethgodin.typepad.com/seths_blog/2008/01/tribal-manageme.html

"People form tribes with or without us. The challenge is to work for the tribe and make it something even better."

Do not try to impose overbearing control over the conversations about your company. Guide and direct, definitely, and set standards of behavior in the communication tools, but don't censor. Ever. Do not censor negative comments. Ever. It totally destroys the concept of a real conversation.

Don't reject anyone who wants to get involved.

Encourage advocacy – anyone you see talking about your company positively should be invited to the "inner circle."

Provide some little extras for that inner circle, such as early access to white papers or additional services at reduced (or no) cost. People like to feel they're getting something others aren't. Highly involved people might get something beyond what regular tribe members get, which is itself a little more than the general viewing audience will get.

You can expect maybe 1-2% of people who know of your company and have some involvement, to be involved in the Tribe as active members.

How to get your tribe's first members

Everyone has a social network, whether it's on the web or not. Most people know a few hundred people and among the couple of hundred you know already, there will be some that will form the seeds of your tribal community. Reach out to them and ask them to reach out to people they know.

Provide them with tools to reach out. Perhaps offer them discount vouchers they can share with their network – discounts that are only valuable when someone does business with your company the first time.

Your passionate customers are going to be those that form the leadership of your tribe. Work with them to help them reach out and share their enthusiasm for the way your business solves their communication/video needs.

7: Why you should have a business blog?

If ever there was a good time to start blogging, it's when everyone else feels the need to focus elsewhere. Blogs have great search engine potential, which will make your business more easily findable on the Internet. Google has a dedicated search engine for blogs. Nino Del Padre of Del Padre Digital, in a Studio Monthly article[54] from January 2009, says that:

> "The original delpadre.com had served my company, Del Padre Digital, well during its lifespan. Some 65 percent of our projects in the last decade were commissioned by clients who found the business online. What's more, our site has long been a showcase of just what our firm could do, a preamble to what would be in store for clients."

Sixty-five percent of their business in the last decade came via their online presence!

A blog is a quick and easy way to have a web presence. They co-exist with your business' more formal site and provide a place to add value. It is also a way to easily add new content to your site regularly.

Regular new content is the key to a successful business blog – one that drives attention to your business so that you can increase it and reach new potential customers. It has to add value. All too many "business blogs" are about the business, from the business' perspective. No matter how great your business is, an endless stream of PR-like posts are not going to help you grow your business. Other than your employees, no-one cares about your business. They care only about what you can do for them.

A post over at Business Logs likens a business blog to the holiday spirit. Not the overt consumerism of the Winter Solstice celebrations but rather the giving side. A good business blog gives useful, valuable information that's relevant to your current and potential customers. You'll spend a lot of time creating great content and then giving it away free in order to enhance your

---

[54] http://www.studiodaily.com/studiomonthly/business/thebiz/

reputation and "trustworthy-ness". This gives potential customers the ability to trust you to deliver their needs on time and budget.

People respond to other people more so than seemingly faceless companies. Back when Robert Scoble was blogging for Microsoft, he personalized Microsoft to the degree that some of my innate antipathy to the company faded: he humanized one of the world's biggest companies.

Although my own business blog is frequently neglected – because I spend time writing books instead of concentrating on the blog – it has worked in my favor a couple of times. Just recently it helped me get a fairly good writing contract simply because it was a very visible and easily accessible way of seeing that I could, indeed, write! It's also helped me get high profile speaking engagements as well as stimulated conversation, and gained me access to the Techdirt consulting community as a contributing expert.

If someone wants to get know about me, my work, or how I think, all they have to do is read the blog[55].

Online reputation, like offline reputation, takes time to build. It's when you take the time and effort to build the reputation and it starts to kick in, that new business will come your way.

That online reputation is going to help when you want to form partnerships with other businesses that will drive work to each other. See "Partner with other business for reciprocal business" earlier in the book.

You'll be great

Video professionals make great bloggers because we're passionate about what we do. We can get into very deep discussions on the relative merits of this camera, that format, or a particular workflow. We love to talk about these things for hours, and if you can talk you can write.

It's a common misconception that writing is difficult. You don't need above average writing skills. If you can talk, you can record it and write down what you said. In fact my *HD Survival Handbook*[56]

---

[55] http://www.philiphodgetts.com

[56] http://www.proappstips.com/HDSurvivalHandbook/

started as a one-day seminar I gave to the Association of Video Professionals[57] a couple of months earlier. That seminar was recorded and that became the basis of the Handbook. As long as you can talk, you can write.

There are services for transcription and software, like Dragon Naturally Speaking[58] (Windows or Mac Bootcamp/Parallels) or MacSpeech Dictate[59] for OS X. MacSpeech uses the same transcription engine as Naturally Speaking, licensed from Dragon. You'll need to train them, and use a high quality mic, but they work for many people.

Don't worry about "the right language." Formal written language makes most people sound stilted and "not real". We want your voice and the real people in your company, so write how you speak. Just check for spelling and basic grammar mistakes. The authentic, direct you, is very appropriate for the "conversation" of the Internet.

You'll have plenty of things to talk about – recycle some of the discussions you've had with clients (educating them) or summarize a discussion on tools or techniques you've had with associates. If you go to free or paid seminars to improve your skills, summarize those and post them. People in their own businesses generally are, or become, good conversationalists. You're constantly talking about your business and how you can add value for your customers. That's all source material for a business blog.

Finally, in my experience, people in production and postproduction businesses tend to be well informed about their crafts. What you say, with your experience in the business, carries weight. Compare a production blog by a film-school student with one by a professional with 20 years of real-world production experience. That carries weight.

---

[57] http://www.aovpros.com/

[58] http://www.nuance.com/naturallyspeaking/

[59] http://www.macspeech.com/

Blogging Tips

Getting started

Business blogging site Business Logs[60] has a six step template[61] for writing blog posts.

Writer Dee Barizo suggests starting with an image. Dee suggests Flickr and stock.xchng[62]. Personally I've purchased quite a few illustrative drawings or pictures from iStockphoto[63] because the prices are reasonable and the service works. If using an image from Flickr be sure to check the specifics of the license granted and stay within that license.

Dee goes on to emphasize the importance of a great title – preferably using "six little words" (coming up shortly) and links to some sites that will help hone the headline skills.

Follow this with a list of your bullet points and then to draft your first draft. Just get in and do it – doesn't matter how bad it is because you'll edit it later. The idea is to explore the ideas you outlined in as much detail as it needs to be.

Before hitting 'Publish' (step 6) re-read the draft one or two times. I prefer to have someone else read over it to ensure it makes sense! Having a trusted editor (however informally) has greatly improved my writing! Use this pass to add any informative subheadings – they help navigate through the story.

Check out the whole article where Dee goes into a lot more depth and links to additional resources.

---

[60] http://www.businesslogs.com

[61] http://www.businesslogs.com/blogging-advice/how_to_write_a_blog_post.php

[62] http://www.sxc.hu/

[63] http://istockphoto.com/index.php

Host your blog on your own domain[64]

There are services at Wordpress.com and Blogger.com where it's simple and easy to set up a blog. They're certainly fast and convenient because everything is managed for you. But, if you are already managing your own domain on a virtual server – a pretty standard basic configuration these days and the minimum standard for a business – then you've got the skills to host your blog on your own domain, or on a sub-domain[65] or a directory off your main domain.

A subdomain currently carries more weight with Google than even a folder on your primary domain. If your site dates back to 2000 or earlier then there is a huge advantage in keeping all the Google references to that domain.

The advantage of hosting the blog on your own domain (or subdomain) is that it will drive up your Google rankings completely legitimately. Your blog's search engine rankings will be added to your main domain – making your commercial website more findable on Google. That's the goal in a post-advertising world.

By trading-off of a little more hands-on management, you get a lot of additional advantages, such as no limits on storage space or bandwidth (up to the limit of your host). When you control your domain you can always add bandwidth or move to a higher capacity server, should the demand grow as a result of your success. You'll also have full access to traffic and website statistics so you can determine where readers are coming from, and where else they go to on your site. You'll also be able to track which are the posts being most read, and most linked to. When you know what works, do more of it!

Finally, being hosted on your own domain makes you look more professional, competent and a company that has substance.

_____

[64] http://performancing.com/12-reasons-to-blog-on-your-own-domain

[65] A subdomain is one that comes before a period ahead of the main domain name. For example theassistanteditor.com is the main domain for some of our software products. The blog that keeps customers, and anyone else interested, informed, is at blog.theassistanteditor.com. Whereas my personal blog is the home page at philiphodgetts.com – there's no site other than the blog.

Note: It is possible to use your own domain name with a Google Blogger account. They have step by step instructions available[66]. You would only do this if your blog was the only thing you were doing. For most, who have some sort of professional website, it's important to keep the blog and commercial site on the same domain name for maximum search engine visibility. A domain cannot easily point to two different servers.

Most hosting companies have the common blogging software WordPress[67] available either pre-installed or with an "easy install" option. Both the hosting companies we use – Media Temple[68] and Dreamhost[69] – have "one-click" installs for WordPress. All our company blogs run on WordPress on the same domain, or in a subdomain, as the primary website.

If the whole "get your own domain" thing sounds too hard for your needs, by all means use blogger or a hosted blog at WordPress[70]. It is better to get your name, and those of your services, "out there" and being heard, than it is to have it on your own domain, it's just not as good as going the whole way.

Update with valuable content regularly

One of the hardest lessons to learn when blogging is to keep up a regular supply of valuable fresh content. Valuable as defined by your readers. More frequent updates are great for your Google ranking and that makes your business easier to find.

The secret to always having something interesting to say is to be passionate about what you do and to simply talk with other people about what you're interested in. If you have an interesting conversation with someone about an aspect of your business, or explain something to a customer during the day, write that up as a post.

---

[66] http://help.blogger.com/bin/answer.py?hl=en&answer=55373

[67] http://wordpress.com/

[68] http://mediatemple.net/

[69] http://www.dreamhost.com/

[70] http://wordpress.com/signup/

As Christ Garrett wrote at the Blog Herald[71]:

> "To begin with you have to think about the mechanics of everything, the technicalities, but the ideas flow along with your initial burst of enthusiasm. After a while the technical geekery becomes automatic and the ideas become the main constraint."[72]

Aim for at least one post a week but post more frequently if you can. It's a discipline and anyone who read my personal blog through 2008 would realize I don't always follow my own excellent advice!

If you suffer from writers block when in the middle of the post – take a break and come back to it. Step away from the keyboard and have a coffee, go for a walk, pet the dog, feed the fish, clean up your desk, whatever. When you come back to finish the post you'll find your mind is clear. Business Logs has a post on the subject[73] that fleshes out these basic ideas.

One theme per post

Keep each post to a single topic or theme and put that theme in the title.

Using a single theme per post makes the content more relevant and that's what Google is looking for to improve your ranking.

If your blogging software supports it, use the optional short description field.

Pick topics that answer questions that are regularly asked

One lesson I learnt in 2008 from Michael Dorausch of Planet Chiropractic[74] was to write blog posts that answer people's questions, so when they search for a question on a search engine, your post comes to the top. Although Michael writes a chiropractic

[71] http://www.blogherald.com/2008/12/31/your-immediate-unlimited-supply-of-blog-post-ideas/

[72] http://www.blogherald.com/2008/12/31/your-immediate-unlimited-supply-of-blog-post-ideas/

[73] http://www.businesslogs.com/blogging-advice/writers_block_in_the_middle_of_a_post.php

[74] http://www.planetc1.com/

blog, he also writes "standard answer" questions that are going to be needed every year.

In our industry, we could post topics like "How to shoot great video over the holiday season" or "What is the best way to shoot at the beach"; "How to light a kids party", etc. (Now there, be creative, don't all do those topics!)

There are certain standard topics that could be covered, including subjects about technologies – "Will the RED camera replace film?"; trends – "How small can an HD camera be and still be useful?"; techniques – "How to speed up rendering of HDV in Final Cut Pro"; or content – "Where is the best online content?".

Write about others

Write about influential or significant contributors to the industry. Most people who are prominent on the Internet have "vanity searches" set up at Technorati[75] or Google Blog Search[76] to alert them to any blog post that might mention themselves, or their important brands or keywords. I have searches for our companies' names, my own name, the radio show I used to host, the names of our software etc – 12 searches across the two services. That way, I usually know whether anything I'm deeply interested in has been mentioned in pretty much any blog.

That is exactly the reason why you should write about others: they will likely see it and that will make them aware of your business. Perhaps they'll write about it, or provide you with a link, if they like what they read.

Consider the "six little words"

George Carlin had is his seven naughty words, well bloggers should know the "six little words"? These words – who, what, when, where, why and how – boost Google ranking. Use them in your subject lines. Never post a subject heading that doesn't use one of the six. There's more on how to best use the six little words coming up.

---

[75] http://technorati.com/

[76] http://blogsearch.google.com/

Look for Hot Trends and google alerts

Google Trends can show you the popularity of searches across their network. With Google Trends you can see the popularity of search terms, and compare popularity of search terms by entering two or more terms separated by commas. It also tells you what are popular searches right now.

Google Insights for Search[77] is another tool from Google. With this you can compare search volume patters across categories, time or regions of the world.

When you see a search becoming popular that fits within your area of expertise, write a post. Be sure to name the post so it reflects the questions being asked. As I write this we're coming up to Inauguration Day 2009 and one of the top 100 searches is for just that: "inauguration day 2009." Immediately I'd be thinking of doing a post on how the Inauguration will be covered on Television. Drilling down to the results page for that search, I see that the New York Times' Bits blog already has an article up "Gearing Up for Mobile Video on Inauguration Day[78]"! (Written the day I'm writing this – Google results are very fast.)

Pick from the "Seven types of posts that attract links"

In another post[79] at Business Logs Dee Barizo lists out seven types of posts that get linked to. While a post production list may not be on Digg's front page any time soon, you can get incoming links for some topics, and that is always helpful in raising your Google ranking.

Make Lists

There's something about a list that attracts attention. The boiling down of wisdom into 5 or 10 "top tips" builds on the desire of most people to want to "cut to the chase" with no wasted fat.

For example, you might want to post "The Top 10 things you need to know when shooting a wedding video" (or child's party, or Graduation or any common event). Or "The five best cameras for

---

[77] http://www.google.com/insights/search/#

[78] http://bits.blogs.nytimes.com/2009/01/05/mobile-video-inauguration-day/

[79] http://www.businesslogs.com/blog-promotion-and-marketing/posts_that_attract_links.php

home video." "Top 10 mistakes Uncle Jack makes with his video." You get the idea.

Make a Glossary

Reference works are great because they have a long life – jargon doesn't change that often. They attract links because people don't know what our technical language means in common terms, therefore they search for the meaning and find your site, and your expertise, waiting for them as a person who "knows it all".

Images and videos

A picture is worth.... putting in your blog posts. Most bloggers don't include images or video and it helps you stand out. (Don't lose out on those image links: make sure they have titles and captions so you pick up image search queries as well.)

Tutorials

People love tutorials and they build your reputation as being knowledgeable about your craft skills. In the article Barizo notes:

> "One SEO expert stated that her favorite method for getting traffic and links was to create an in-depth tutorial and then promote it in social media.
>
> Relevant tutorials get lots of links because many internet users are looking for content that shows them how to do a certain task. They want the content to show them step by step how to accomplish their task."

Metaphors

As the author explains it, metaphors are great because they shake up our perception. Topics like "Monty Python's secret to selling video online" or "The Harry Potter style of video postproduction[80]".

Humor and stories

If you're a genuinely good storyteller, or are truly funny in your writing, these are great tools to use on your business blog. Do not write comedy or stories if you're not that good at it. Instead write from your heart about things you know about.

------

[80] I have no idea what the content of that post would be, but I'd read it for sure!

Write Multiple posts at a time

Sometimes you're on a roll with ideas and it all just flows, so you end up with two or three items in the day and then nothing for a day or so. With people likely to be reading on at the same part of their day every day, and for the benefit of your Google index, regular new information is a good thing. So, when you're on a roll, do those extra posts but save them as a draft. Then, on a day when you're idea or time poor, just publish one of your already-written pieces. Use it as a way of evening out your productivity and capitalizing on those times when ideas flow.

Further Reading

7 Stealth Publish for WordPress Uses to Consider[81]

Writing for Subscriber Heaven: More of the Same but Better[82]

Guest Posting 101[83]

---

[81] http://seo2.0.onreact.com/7-stealth-publish-for-wordpress-uses-to-consider

[82] http://seo2.0.onreact.com/7-writing-for-subscriber-heaven-more-of-the-same-but-better

[83] http://www.businesslogs.com/blog-promotion-and-marketing/how-to-write-effective-guest-posts.php

8:   Maximize your visibility on the Internet

SEO (Search Engine Optimization) aims to place you as high in the search engine rankings as you possibly can get, at least for the search terms you care about. You will know the search terms people are using to find you from your analytics software. In fact, before you can optimize your site for optimal search engine results (see next section) you need good, solid information on what people do when they come to your site; where they go and how long they stay.

You can experiment and see what works and what doesn't, but before you can get started you need that data. While there are many web statistics analysis packages available, Google Analytics is free. Because it is free there are many tutorials and books on how to optimize your site using the Data from Google Analytics.

Web stats analysis 'software' takes the raw information that's present in your web server's logs and turns it into statistics and graphs that show you exactly how people navigate your site, where they come from, where they go to, where they are in the world, and whatever action they take on your site. Web stats software either needs installing on your server so you can access it through a browser, or you need to download your server logs to be processed by desktop software.

Google Analytics requires a small snippet of code to be added to each page and nothing more.

Your business name and website URL

I'm fairly lucky that 'Philip Hodgetts' – indeed 'Hodgetts' itself – is not a very common name. There are only two entries for the family name above my personal blog on a search on my family name alone.

But poor John Smith's Video and Postproduction is going to have a very hard time standing out and being found on the Internet. While it may be too late to change your business name – there is a lot of entrenched goodwill to an existing name – if you're thinking about updating or modernizing your company name think of one that will index as being fairly unique. The goal is to have your company site come up at the top (or in the top three) on a search for the name. If it doesn't you need to work on keywords and SEO optimization until it does.

Likewise you want your site to come up in the top rankings for the keywords you choose to describe your business (see below).

Website URL

In almost all cases, the domain for a business must be in .com. In a video-centric business you may get away with the more expensive .tv for your domain, but browsers (at least on OS X) will assume any URL typed in without the top level domain is .com.

Avoid using dashes to separate words. It confuses people because you always have to spell out that there is a dash and where it is. People now assume that there is no punctuation in a URL and default to not using any. Use a dash if you have to, to be in .com, but be very aware that people will go to a version without a dash.

Buy up the "typo" domains near your own. I'm not a big fan of buying up my domains in every top level: I settle for .com and don't bother with .net, .org etc. I am a big fan of buying up similar or nearby names. I confess, I originally only purchased proappstips.com because the guys who had proapptips.com hadn't protected against my typo and I went to a non-existent website. Now we get more traffic than they do.

Domains are cheap, as long as you're not buying from old-school registrars like Network Solutions. (No link because they have, in my own opinion, some unsavory business practices.) We buy through GoDaddy.com where a .com domain, with tax and fees, is about $10 a year. I would not host there, because I think there are better deals elsewhere, like Dreamhost.com or 1and1.com.

> **Tip:** Have the person who supports your website make sure that http://intelligentassistance.com works as well as http://www.intelligentassistance.com. This is usually a setting at the ISP, but if varies according to the hosting company.

Install Google Analytics

Install Google Analytics[84] as you're setting up the website. Google Analytics is free. It will provide you with an enormous amount of useful information. You can use that information to optimize your website. For example, once you know how people are finding your site you can improve your appeal to those sources. You'll know what search terms show your program's site in the top results. This information is doubly useful if you ever decide to participate in Google's (paid) Adwords[85] program because you'll know what search terms – that's the Adsense keywords – you should bid on. We discuss using Adsense later.

Conversion Rate

An important piece of information you'll learn from the analysis is your take rate, drop out rate, or conversion rate. Whatever you call it, it tells you how people behave on the site. It will tell you where people stop taking any action. For example, do they follow the link to your "sign up for our email" entry and then go no further? If so, maybe you should consider having the email signup as part of the home page (or every page). Make it easy for people to do what you want them to do.

You will no doubt want to experiment with different designs, comparing the success rate of your desired action – from Google Analytics – for different copy or designs of the page. Scott Buresh has an article on The Importance of Website Conversion[86] that will help expand your understanding.

Another place you might look for information is in the Optimizing Landing Pages for Lead Generation and Conversion[87] webinar at Hubspot. The slides are also available.

---

[84] http://www.google.com/analytics/

[85] http://www.google.com/intl/en_us/ads/ads_1.html

[86] http://digitalproducer.digitalmedianet.com/articles/viewarticle.jsp?id=680502

[87] http://www.hubspot.com/archive/optimizing-landing-pages

Bounce Rate

Particularly relevant to getting the maximum benefit is your "bounce rate". Yes, another piece of jargon, but it's important. A "bounce" is where someone arrives on a page on your site – by following a link or search result – and does nothing before heading off to another site. They don't fill in a form, they don't follow a link, they just move on to somewhere else. (You will get information on where else they're going.) Of course there will always be some bounce rate because people arrive on a web page and then realize it wasn't what they expected. Google have some suggestions on reducing your bounce rate[88].

Google Analytics will also tell you how long they stayed on the page before heading off, so you can gain some sense of whether they at least read your material, or not.

Search Engine Optimization

SEO is a huge field these days and you can pay a lot for specialists. (If you are thinking of paying someone for this service, consult Questions to ask before hiring a Search Engine Marketing Company [89].)

Regularly updated, quality content is one of the most important factors in how easily your project will be found in search engines. That's why it's important to have your blog on the same domain, or in a subdomain of that domain. Subdomains – that is subdomain.yourdomain.com – are counted as being part of the main site in Google's rankings.

I thoroughly recommend the Hubspot Internet Marketing Blog[90] (correctly placed on a subdomain from the main site). They also have a number of free recordings of webinars they've created. Another useful resource is an article by Daniele Bazzano at Master New Media[91] (also recommended) called How To Make My

---

[88] http://googleblog.blogspot.com/2009/02/stop-bouncing-tips-for-website-success.html

[89] http://www.bluecatdesign.com/bcat/seo-how-to-choose.html

[90] http://blog.hubspot.com/

[91] http://www.masternewmedia.org/

Site Findable And Visible Inside Google SERPs? Here Is The Google SEO Formula And Visibility Toolkit[92]. The article *is* longer than the title, with great information, including additional reference materials.

While it takes time to learn SEO, and I consider myself to still be a learner, the investment of time to learn is going to be worth it in building your client base.

The quick guide to SEO

Follow these simple guidelines and you'll get the quickest bang-for-buck for time invested in SEO. As I've said, SEO can be almost a full-time career, but you don't have to be an expert to give your company's site a boost in the search engines, and that's never a bad thing.

This guide covers what you need to do on a single page: repeat across your entire site.

Know, and use, your keywords

The keywords are the search terms people might use to find your site. You already have a clue what terms people are searching for when they find your site, thanks to Google Analytics. These words are a useful starting point, but you will need to build on them.

Think about the terms your potential clients will use to get the result they're after. Note that: get the result *they're* after. So, "video production" isn't necessarily a good keyword, whereas "company video", "video-based training", "family DVD", "conference video", are much better because they target the result people are searching for. They don't want editing facilities, they want edited video – video programming or entertainment. Do not confuse the two. You'll get much better results with your keywords when they're framed from the perspective of the solution than the problem. For more detailed info, read: Detailed Internet Marketing Keyword Tips[93].

---

[92] http://www.masternewmedia.org/how-to-make-my-site-findable-and-visible-inside-google-serps/

[93] http://www.hubspot.com/MarketingTips/Internet-Marketing-Keywords/tabid/8625/Default.aspx

Google Trends

A very useful way to find search terms that people are using to find business like yours is to explore using <u>Google Trends</u>[94]. Google Trends shows how often a particular search term is entered relative to the total search volume across various regions of the world, and in various languages.

The information on popularity of searches is graphed over time, but the most valuable usage is to see how popular given search terms are, or to compare two or more search terms for popularity. A comparison of "Conference Video" against "Video for Conference" shows that 'Conference Video' is way, way hotter than 'Video for Conference.'[95]

Popularity of search terms is broken down by region, city and language and it is possible to refine the main graph by region and time.

Put your keywords in the title of the page

The title of the page shows, usually, across the top of the browser window (unless the browser places the tabs at the top, like Safari 4 and Google Chrome). Put some of your keywords in the title in a natural way. For example, "How a great *conference video* will help stimulate your sales team" would make a great page title and carry a lot more SEO weight than the same content and a title of "Video production for conferences."

For a fuller understanding of using keywords in page titles, read <u>Why a Web Page By Any Other Title Would Not Rank As Well</u>[96].

Put your keywords in the URL of the page

Apparently Google and the other search engines also index the actual URL, so think about how you can structure your site so that keywords end up in the URL. For example, for our consultancy business – part of Intelligent Assistance, Inc. – the URL should (and will when we combine the sites) read:

---

[94] http://www.google.com/trends

[95] I had not performed the Google Trends test on these terms until after I had written the earlier paragraph.

[96] http://blog.hubspot.com/blog/tabid/6307/bid/1211/A-Web-Page-By-Any-Other-Title-Would-Not-Rank-As-Well.aspx

http://www.intelligentassistance.com/post-production_workflow/ Final_Cut_Pro_Workflow.html or similar. "Production Workflow" and "Final Cut Pro Workflow" are both relevant keywords.

If you don't manage your own website, talk to the person who does and structure the site to take advantage of the keywords in the structure of the site, which will bring them into the URL.

Put the Keywords in your page metadata

The page metadata is entered when the page is authored and was originally designed to have some brief keywords that described the page. Clearly that's an invitation to add your keywords there, and you absolutely should. Put in the keyword phrase or keywords that go with that content. Add as much as necessary but no more.

For more detailed info, read Hubspot's Understanding the Magic of Meta-Data[97].

Use Keywords in your H1 text

The largest title on each page will usually be tagged as H1 (Largest size paragraph text). H1 text is usually the title of an article or something else in large type on the page. Google and other search engines put more emphasis on the words in the H1 text than the smaller text, so make sure your keyword or phrase is there as much as possible, without it seeming forced.

Write with your keywords in mind

Although the search engines put more weight on the H1 text, they also look at the content on the page to determine what the page is about. Putting keywords in the body text signals to the search engine that the page is, indeed, about the subject of the keywords.

Some "experts" say (and I sure won't argue) that you should use your keyword(s) anywhere from 4-6 times on the page; other "experts" propose 10-12 times, but that would be hard to do and still write naturally. Making the page readable and useful to the reader is more important than stuffing it with keywords, so write naturally.

---

[97] http://blog.hubspot.com/blog/tabid/6307/bid/29/SEO-For-Small-Business-Executives-Understanding-The-Magic-Of-Meta-Data.aspx

Use a lot of images

Google looks at images as well as the text. You'll want to give your images a title and (less importantly) a caption. Preferably put one of your keywords in the image file name or the image title.

Images can come from your own shoots or stock images. Whenever you shoot a project take a digital still camera with you – it doesn't have to be a full-blown DSLR when a snapshot will do. Keep representative stills from interesting postproduction projects, particularly where effects are composited and a new reality constructed. Use those images to illustrate your website and the stories there.

An article that will help optimize the results from image is 7 Simple Image SEO Best Practices that Lead to the Top of Google Image Search[98].

Monitor the results

My friend, Brad Wright, developer of DVDxDV[99] and Veescope Live, Veescope Key and Veescope Signals, is more advanced than I am at using SEO to market his software products. He tells me he can attribute which of the various testimonial videos on his site contribute most to sales. He knows this because he monitors how people are moving through his site and where they go after they watch a testimonial video. (Brad turned me on to *Web Design for ROI*[100] as the source of his newly gained understanding.)

Whenever you make a change to your site, take the time to examine what affect it has had on sales and the things that lead to sales: more time reviewing information about your company and projects, placing orders etc.

---

[98] http://seo2.0.onreact.com/7-simple-image-seo-best-practices-that-lead-to-the-top-of-google-image-search

[99] http://www.dvdxdv.com/

[100] http://www.amazon.com/gp/product/0321489829

Monitor your page rank

After you've made these changes across your site, check your page rank to see how much you've risen through the ranks.

Search on your keywords and see where you come in the rankings. Check those sites that come in higher than you and look at their page titles, and articles to look for clues on how to improve your own ranking.

For more details, read this article about The Importance of Google Page Rank[101].

Create smart internal links

When you're cross-linking within your site, be smart about it. Add links to the words that are most relevant to the topic at hand. Links are links, and they carry weight for SEO even when they're within the domain.

This version of the link is less valuable because it links from irrelevant words:

> "For more information see my article[102] 'What are the different types of metadata we can use in production and post production?'"

Instead, attach the link to the words that are more relevant to the site:

> "For more information see my article 'What are the different types of metadata we can use in production and post production?'"

Build links to, and from, your site

The number of links that Google considers to be 'quality' links is one of the most important factors in your page rank. Using links as a way of determining a site's importance was Google's original innovation.

---

[101] http://blog.hubspot.com/blog/tabid/6307/bid/45/The-Importance-of-Google-PageRank-A-Guide-For-Small-Business-Executives.aspx

[102] http://www.philiphodgetts.com/?p=165

The links must be 'quality' – that is they should not be faked or built up in some phony way. They should come from relevant sites only.

Read this article to understand the importance of links to your website: Link Building for SEO / Internet Marketing[103] and read this article for more details on why to link to others: No Website is an Island – How and Why to Link to Others[104].

A site with only incoming links will rank higher than a site that has no links, but a site with large numbers of incoming links and a lot of outgoing links tells Google that this is a "reference" site and therefore should rank higher in search results, because it's more likely to have useful information for any given search undertaken.

Avoid Pitfalls

Google is a hard mistress. If you should break any of their (mostly) unspoken and undocumented rules you can suddenly lose your entire page rank, or drop several hundred pages in that rank. A sudden drop in ranking is effectively being invisible, because people mostly only look at the first page of search results.

Some lesser traps for the new SEO practitioner can dramatically limit your success with search engines. Check out hubspot.com's Why You're Not Getting Enough Respect from Search Engines[105] to get a clearly understand of what you may be doing wrong, or simply to avoid falling into the common traps. Another article that will help avoid mistakes that cost you ranking is Top 10 Most Egregious SEO Mistakes[106].

---

[103] http://www.hubspot.com/MarketingTips/Link-Building-SEO/tabid/16602/Default.aspx

[104] http://blog.hubspot.com/blog/tabid/6307/bid/235/No-Website-Is-An-Island-Why-and-How-To-Link-To-Others.aspx

[105] http://blog.hubspot.com/blog/tabid/6307/bid/13/Internet-Marketing-Why-You-re-Not-Getting-Enough-Respect-From-Search-Engines.aspx

[106] http://blog.hubspot.com/blog/tabid/6307/bid/4040/Top-10-Most-Egregious-SEO-Mistakes.aspx

Grade your website frequently

Take advantage of free resources to grade your website, starting with Website Grader[107] (free tool) to evaluate the marketing effectiveness of your website. It gives tips on what you can change on your site to improve your website's marketing effectiveness.

If you want to see your site as a search engine sees it then SEO-browser.com will be helpful. It shows what the search engines are seeing and how your site ranks.

Another site that will help you interpret how well you're doing is Smart Page Rank[108].

Further reading

There are a lot of (mostly) free resources for further improving your SEO skills, such as 10 Great SEO Sites[109].

Another deeper resource is How to SEO Your Site in Less Than 60 Minutes although I'm pretty sure it'll take a whole lot longer than an hour.

If you want the good word from Yahoo's SEO Manager, Tony Adams[110] did an interview for Mixergy.

Other articles you might find useful are:

How To Make My Site Findable And Visible Inside Google SERPs?[111]

Online Key Performance Indicators:[112] Select And Identify Your Strategic KPI To Measure Your Website Progress

---

[107] http://www.websitegrader.com/

[108] http://www.smartpagerank.com/

[109] http://www.46schoolstreet.com/10-great-seo-sites.html

[110] http://blog.mixergy.com/basic-seo/

[111] http://www.masternewmedia.org/how-to-make-my-site-findable-and-visible-inside-google-serps/

[112] http://www.masternewmedia.org/online-key-performance-indicators-select-and-identify-your-strategic-kpi-to-measure-your-website-progress/

For video search, Mastering New Media's article **Online** Video SEO: How To Make Your Video Content More Visible On Major Search Engines[113] will be helpful

Other traffic building tips

Everything that builds your company brand will ultimately help your company be found by search engines.

Write for others

Offer to write guest posts on other people's blogs or articles for their websites. My articles are published across a number of sites on the Internet, including magazine websites. Some have been translated to multiple European languages. Every one of them builds my visibility and increases the likelihood that someone will find me or one of our businesses.

Write reviews at Amazon

Whenever you finish a book, write a review at Amazon and use your company name.

Even content posts on Craig's List can drive traffic to your site, although I'm not sure what relevant content you would contribute to that location!

Have many calls to action

From the very first day you roll out the website for your business, make it more than simply a static billboard. From day one you'll want to encourage people to subscribe to your blog.

The next call to action should be to subscribe to an email newsletter that you will send out every month (no more frequently) that summarizes what's new in your business that helps customers achieve their goals faster, better or cheaper. If you haven't got something new every month, get working on that!

We've already talked about two ways to get people to sign up – a newsletter or blog feed – but don't let them be the only ways. You can legitimately ask for an email address for some type of special

[113] http://www.masternewmedia.org/online-video-seo-how-to-make-your-video-content-more-visible/

content – perhaps a series of tutorials; or a "Making of" showing how effects were put together for one or more of your projects. Use the approach "For our inner circle of friends – those who share their email address with us – we have this extra something."

Converting visitors to buyers

The most important tool you will need for optimizing your website for converting visitors to customers is the reports from your analytics software. I've advocated Google Analytics because it is free and provides good quality information. Because it's free, Google Analytics is become ' the standard' for most people's website analysis needs and therefore there is a lot of on-line and print support for how to use the reported results.

As you develop your website and optimize the results, you will use these results constantly to determine how the site is performing. Each change will be monitored to see if it improves (or the opposite) your conversion rate.

Think like the customer

Why are your customers at your site? Why are they there? What do they want?

Does your site, pitch and copy make sense? Is it easy to understand by someone who understands nothing about your business, or the process of creating video?

Does it look easy? Each 'next step' should be very easy and non-threatening.

Do they trust you? What is your reputation? (Avoid deals that are "too good to be true" even if you can deliver, as that always makes people edgy.)

Create conversion opportunities everywhere

If you're selling something, put an opportunity for more information, or a purchase, anywhere it's appropriate. It shouldn't dominate, nor should it be hard to find.

Such conversion opportunities can go on the home page, product pages, information pages, or even blog posts (although I personally don't do that as my blog is personal not corporate).

Each time a person takes one more step in learning more, watching a testimonial video or downloading a trial, they're committing further toward the purchase or to contacting you for a production quote. Anywhere you want someone to do something, make that thing easy to do.

Watch your Analytics for pages with a high bounce rate. Pages where people abandon their quest – take no action other than leaving your site – need work. You'll need to analyze what's wrong with that page, and change it to make the response better.

Special reports

Write white papers on the industry. Adapt them from your blog posts and make them available as a downloadable PDF. To get the download customers have to fill out a very short interest form – name, email address and, maybe, a checkbox for their type of interest. No more.

With each download you have another customer who's taken a step closer to buying services from you.

There are all sorts of white papers you can write: "How to order video services"; "ROI from branded video content"; "How effects are done", etc. An educated client will cause you less frustration and they'll understand what value you bring, having sold themselves on your services.

Free consultation

Everyone loves free and how better to engage a potential production customer with free consultations. There is a perception of value for the potential customer and certainly there is the potential for a sale for you.

Don't offer a single "take it or leave it" consultation. With each page's content, make an appropriate pitch for a free consultation. If you're talking about titling on an information page, the free consultation pitch would be "Want to improve your titles, find out how with a free consultation on how you benefit from great titles."

On a page about how branded content brings benefits to companies, the pitch might be "Find out how branded content will work for you in a free consultation with our branded content specialists."

Keep required actions simple

The actions you want your potential customers to take should be simple and clear. Wherever possible include the words "click here to…" (although for SEO purposes you'll have the link attached to the "to…" part, not on the 'click here'.

Link off both images and text. Provide a link from the text and if there is a related image, link from the image as well. Potential customers can click on either.

Action oriented and Positive

Links should always be action focused: 'Download our free white papers'; 'sign up for our free seminar'.

In the invitation, include the benefit to the client of doing so. "Download our free white paper on xyz to improve your wxy".

Make it pop

Your calls to action should be graphically obvious and eye catching. Vonage are the kings of getting attention on a page with their bright orange invitations to action.

Match landing page and offer

For each offer you're making, link to a specific landing page with all the details: what's in it for the customer, what's the offer, and a big prominent action button!

Make it pretty and simple

Landing pages for offers should be simply designed – avoid clutter and minimize navigation elements – and use graphics for visual appeal. Solid blocks of text are hard to read and put people off.

Keep it short

Offers should be as short as possible. Hubspot cite an example where simplifying the offer increased the conversion rate from 32% to 53%. This result was achieved by reducing the text describing the offer by about half and reducing the requested information fields from 12 to 4 (two of which are the email address – for confirmation of accuracy). Less is often more.

Keep the form above the 'fold'

In web design work the 'fold' is the amount of screen viewed in a default browser view. It parallels the thinking that the top half of a newspaper is more valuable than the bottom half because people tend to fold their paper in half.

In web design, anything that requires scrolling down is likely to get missed, so NEVER put the action button or entry form anywhere that requires scrolling down. The whole offer should be visible in the default view, without scrolling. These days the assumption is that people browse on screens at least 1024 x 768. Design so that your content fits within that display size – after taking out the surround for the browser, the browser's menus and the system menus.

Be reasonable what you ask for

People have a graduated fear of intrusion. Receiving email is fairly non-obtrusive, so people will give out their email address. Fewer people will give out a phone number or address; even fewer will give out credit card details without a very clear understanding of why; and no thinking person would enter their full social security number on a web form except for very specific circumstances.

The less you ask for the more likely it is that someone will give you their information and make the step toward becoming a customer.

Avoid the 'cancel' or 'clear' button

Don't make it easy for people to abandon a form they've already entered text into. Simply use a "continue" button to move to the next step. Providing a Clear or Cancel button makes it that much easier for people to avoid the next step – continuing.

People who don't want to continue can use their browser's back button, follow another link or abandon the site, or even close the window. They have enough ways to back out, you don't need to make it easier for them.

Follow up

When you get email addresses from people looking at your 'extra content for our special friends' (those tutorials, making of or facility tour videos) or from people downloading a trial version/trailer of something you sell electronically, follow up a few days later. Three to five days after the download is optimal. Less than three days and it appears you're pushy; beyond a week and people have tended to forget why they ever downloaded the trailer or trial version.

If you don't follow up, you're probably wasting most of your online efforts. Few people will bring production work to you based on your web site alone. You're looking to convert them into a free consultation, or other way of getting them talking with you about their needs.

The *offers* you should make

We've already talked about free white papers, tutorials, videos and seminars you can organize locally.

Always keep focused on the WIIFM – What's In It For Me – for the customer.

Free trials work. Offer as may free trials as you can. For subscription content or many software products free trials are easy. For video production and post production, a little more difficult but you could offer a free hour of post or, as I've mentioned earlier, consultation on their project.

Money back guarantees work as well. We offered complete satisfaction guarantees on our Intelligent Assistant products. Of the many tens of thousands we sold, we refunded exactly two, because the Intelligent Assistants were not "like" what the customer was used to and expected. Complete, 100% money back guarantees give people peace of mind and help make a sale. Do not offer one unless you plan to follow through. People did not have to have a reason other than "I don't think it gave me value" to get a refund on a purchase from us. We continue this policy with our Assisted Editing software products, particularly where we can't offer a trial or demonstration version.

A perceived step up in value from a white paper is a "kit." You might create your own "Commissioning a video production" kit. This would be a combination of a couple of relevant white papers repurposed; some work sheets to help people determine their production goals, and maybe a budgeting worksheet.

A kit is another offer you can make in return for contact details and a little information about the potential client.

Six Little Words

George Carlin had his seven dirty words but in optimizing for search engines, there are six little words that have a big impact. Anyone that's worked with, or as, a journalist will recognize:

Who?

What?

When?

Where?

Why?

and the non-conformist, How?

So when you're marketing a production business and are writing for the company blog use topics like:

"Why we chose Sony's EX-1" instead of "Our new EX-1"

"What opportunities arise when Digital Cinemas are common?" instead of "Cinema changing to Digital Projection."

"How high quality graphics add customer appeal" not "See our graphics reel."

If it comes to announcing a new person or position change, choose "Who's taking responsibility for keeping our gear running?" instead of the typical "Bob Smith joins us as or new technical guru" or "Bob Smith appointed to Head Engineering."

Framing the post or article or other writing you use for promotion this way helps frame the story in active terms, and focused on the benefit to the customer – the sizzle of the steak on the grill – instead of the features – it's a steak!

These words work, because they parallel the way people search. When people are searching for an answer they type in a question.

So play to this by writing posts that answer common questions people ask about your business. If you're the only person writing on the subject, it'll come up at the top of search results – because it's the best match. You'll also get more links to the article as it's a reference source for anyone researching that subject.

Over the last dozen years or so, I've written many articles, often on fairly narrow subjects. To this day if you type in "What is displacement mapping in After Effects?" my article from 1999 – put up at CreativeCOW.net in 2004, is the top hit. The SEO-friendly title was selected "naively" as there was no Search Engines to optimize back then. However, as I review the titles of articles I've written, a good portion use the Six Little Words approach.

Keep the Six Little Words in mind when you're thinking up titles for videos and projects. It's not always going to be possible to work one into the program name but "Where's Waldo?" is a whole lot more search engine friendly than "Waldo's wild trips!" Considering the search engine potential for video, film or other media project is important when searches on YouTube now account for 25% of total Google searches![114]

Here's some inspiration from Business Logs for the Six Little Words.[115]

Use YouTube (etc.) as your calling card

YouTube is a great free hosting service. If you're producing testimonial videos, or other material you're using on your site to promote your services, you should upload any that are publicly available (i.e. not part of your "give us your email address and we'll show you more" content) to YouTube.

Of course, you don't want to limit yourself to just YouTube since there are nearly 200 video sharing sites (although you won't want to worry about most of them). To make it easy to get your content pushed out across the most important sites, create your own accounts at each site, then use TubeMogul[116] to push to multiple

---

[114] http://www.techcrunch.com/2008/12/18/comscore-youtube-now-25-percent-of-all-google-searches/

[115] http://www.businesslogs.com/blogging-advice/increase_search_traffic_6_keywords.php

[116] http://www.tubemogul.com/

sites at once. You upload each video to TubeMogul and it gets pushed out to all sites you've decided to be part of.

TubeMogul also aggregates the statistics and analytics for your videos wherever they're seen so you don't have to go track at each of the services individually.

Create your own channels on YouTube

One problem with using YouTube to distribute your marketing content is that the URLs for movies are to regular YouTube pages where 'similar' videos will be offered to your viewers that may have no relevance for your potential customers. Instead you want to create a custom channel for your content. Your YouTube channel is actually a customized version of your User Profile page. YouTube creates a user profile page when you first become a member of the site. The default is bland so you'll want to customize it before spreading the URL around.

Log into your User Profile page, hereafter called your channel, by clicking the My Account link at the top of any YouTube page. Scroll down to the Channel Settings section.

Once there you can customize the information under the following links:

Channel Info: This is where you make the profile page a channel page by entering a new title and description for your channel. You can choose a video to use for your profile picture, or the last video you uploaded will be used.

Channel Design: You can choose a new color scheme; hide or show various page elements as well as upload a background image (logo anyone?) for your channel page. This is where you match the look and feel of your channel page to be as close to the design of your company website and business cards.

Personal Information: Feel free to share as much 'personal' (i.e. company information if this is a company channel) information as you want.

Location Information: City, zip code and country would be reasonable for a company channel; home town not so much.

Channel URL: This is where you recover your channel URL

Important: Don't forget to click the Update Channel button after making any changes or you'll lose the changes you've made.

As this is a company site you'll probably want to hide your 'age' in the channel as it won't be relevant. Do this in the Personal Info link and select the Do not Display your Age on your Public Profile option.

Click on Update Channel when you're done.

Viewing and using your channel

The direct URL for your channel, now customized to be an ambassador for your business, will be available under the Channel URL link. This is the link you will distribute to people.

Visitors to your channel can find out the videos you've uploaded and which videos are tagged as your favorites.

Your channel not only contains your videos in a look and feel like your company site, but it also has information about the company (user); a link to subscribe to the channel, links to connect to the user, channels the company is watching and who else is subscribed to this channel.

YouTube also enables comments on your channel. It is the central way for YouTube viewers to connect with your company.

Your goal is to get subscribers to your channels, so as you push out new material, they're notified. Use this to start building a following for your company and raise your profile on the Internet (and therefore be easier to find in search engines).

9: Sell

I am not for a moment going to attempt to tell you how to replace all the sales and advertising you currently do for your business. Rather, I want to look at what being a good salesperson requires and how you can add Internet advertising to your promotional and sales mix.

What you need before you get more customers

According to Seth Godin, there are three things you need if you want more customers[117]:

1. A group of potential customers who are not your current customers that you can identify and reach;

2. A group of people with a problem that you can provide a solution for (preferably the same group as point one); and

3. A group of potential customers with desire and money to solve that problem.

It's relatively easy to find any one of the three; quite easy to find potential customers with two needs, but the real gold is when we find potential customers with all three: an identifiable and reachable group of people with a business communication problem that you can solve, and who are prepared to pay for the solution.

Keep this in mind when trying to find new customers.

---

[117] http://sethgodin.typepad.com/seths_blog/2009/02/three-things-you-need-if-you-want-more-customers.html

Turn into a great salesperson

A common misconception is that the job of a salesperson is to trick people into buying stuff they really don't need. Nothing could be further from the truth. Truly professional salespeople match the needs of their customer with the products they represent. Good salespeople never try to sell customers something that won't meet their needs, or is beyond the cost benefit the customer will receive.

The job of sales is not just the conversion of enquirers into customers, although that certainly should be part of what you do. Sales is pervasive everywhere you want to get something done. You need to 'sell' other people in your company on the equipment you might buy, on the direction the company is going, etc. (If you are President or CEO you still need to sell your vision to bring people along with you.)

Feedback and measurement

Street vendor sales folk know exactly how much they've made each day – the cash in their hand less the expenses. In a more brand-focused business, where projects take longer to sell but are higher priced sales, you need to know what works for you and what doesn't.

This means measuring everything and recording changes. In the section on being visible on the Internet we talked about how valuable Google Analytics can be. You will be able to measure the amount of web traffic that is provided from every ad impression. You'll know if your website copy converts that interest into an action, and what actions have been taken.

The best thing about web advertising is that, unlike other forms of advertising, the results are traceable. If no one follows links in your search advertising to your site, you clearly need to change your pitch, your keywords or your campaign strategy.

Have input into product and service offerings

If this is your business then you'll have a big say in the product offerings, but remember, no matter how you structure your products or services, or services as products, if you're not offering something that people want to buy, you won't have a business.

It's all too easy to get caught up on how cool the technology is, or how the latest-and-greatest widget will 'change the industry', but if your clients aren't there, you've made a huge business mistake and no matter what you do in 'sales' it still won't sell.

It's the benefit you're selling

Often expressed as "sell the sizzle, not the steak", what you are really selling is a benefit to the customer. You are not selling the service or product your company provides, you are selling the benefit to the customer.

Remember right back at the beginning of the book I said that your only role in business is to make money for other people? Having that focus from the start will greatly benefit sales.

Pete Warden on his PeteSearch blog talks about making the product the star[118] and in the context he was writing – a guide for technology startups – that makes sense. Don't just talk about your new product, demonstrate it. But if you demonstrate the features, people won't get it: if you demonstrate the benefit, they will.

Be a fan

If you try to sell something you don't believe in 100% it will show and you won't be as successful. You need to believe that what you offer is absolutely the best solution for the customer. If you do not believe that, do NOT make the sale. Your customer won't be happy when they realize, and your reputation will suffer.

I have been a huge fan of everything we've **ever** created. The only time I was convinced that our Intelligent Assistants were "only" one of many good training solutions, I found my desire to push and promote lost a little edge and enthusiasm, which was a pity because they were the absolute best way to gain the working

---

[118] http://petewarden.typepad.com/searchbrowser/2009/01/what-makes-a-great-salesman.html

knowledge people needed, in the most convenient and effective method.

Needless to say, this book is absolutely the best package of knowledge you'll need to grow your production or post production business in the circumstances of the New Now.

How to be more persuasive

People are not logical. Frequently they can have all the facts and still not make a decision to buy production or postproduction services that you know will provide them with huge benefit.

That's because people do not respond to facts. People have opinions and facts don't tell people why their opinion is wrong. People do not like being wrong, so trying to convince them with facts would be forcing them to admit, in a way, that they were wrong. When presented with information that is challenging their belief, people tend to lower the value of the source of that information, without ever considering it could be right.

People love stories. Stories work on the right side of the brain where the listener lives the experience. People can identify with the hero or become the hero in their own minds, when you tell the story right!

Having lived and breathed the story, they start to apply the story to their own context. This is why customers love to hear success stories from their suppliers: that they can convert into experiences they could have.

The crucial factor is to get the right story to the right audiences. You should, by now, have stories to tell about your business. You can now choose which story the current "audience" (of one or more) will most relate to.

There is more on the subject of being persuasive from Stephen Denning, author of _The Secret Language of Leadership_[119], in an interview with Andrew Warner[120] at Mixergy.

---

[119] http://www.amazon.com/gp/product/0787987891

[120] http://blog.mixergy.com/persuasive-denning/

Display advertising vs Search advertising

Overall, display advertising – banners basically – is shrinking as a portion of all Internet advertising. This is partly due to a shrinking advertiser budgets, but also because display advertising does not work most of the time. People are getting so sick of viewing ugly, intrusive banner advertising that they are running ad-blocking software in their browser or they simply tune out ads.

For me, running with ad blocking is the only way I can stand to surf the Internet. Without it, my eyes start to bleed after an hour or so! So, don't waste money on banner advertising. The only banner ads that do have any positive effect are brand building, not action oriented. Right now we're building our brand online, through our business blog, social media and all the things we've been talking about up to here. We don't need relatively expensive display advertising.

Because display advertising is becoming so unpopular, and because there are fewer advertisers than ever, the cost of display advertising is getting lower. Unfortunately display advertising is usually charged on the old model: you pay for display not for action. Even if no-one clicks on the ad, you still pay full rate.

While display advertising has been shrinking as a portion of all Internet advertising, Search advertising is growing. Search advertising is also the lowest risk investment in advertising possible: if no-one clicks on a link you don't pay as the advertiser, giving you the freedom to experiment and change your advertising copy.

Adsense, Adwords

<u>Adwords</u>[121] is Google's ad-placing program. People with something to sell take out Adwords. Website owners can embed Adsense[122] on their website and get revenue from clicks on the ads on their site. Adsense places relevant ads on sites by examining the content of each page and selecting ads relevant to the content.

All ads placed by Adsense are from the ads in the Adwords network. Unless you have a site with very significant traffic there is little value in Adsense for the site. Adsense on your corporate site will send the wrong message about your company – that your company will do anything to make a buck in the short term. That's not a good message to be sending out.

So we're talking about Adwords from this point on.

What are Adwords?

Google Adwords allows people in any sized business to purchase highly targeted ads regardless of budget. Adwords ads are pay-per-click: no clicks on your ads, no payment to Google (and sadly, no new business for you). Adwords ads are displayed beside search results on Google, and many other sites through Adsense.

Adwords ads are built around keywords. When creating your text-only ad, you choose keywords that will be used to trigger the display of your ad. When someone searches for your keywords, or the keywords are relevant for an Adsense site, your ad will be displayed. Advertisers set monthly or daily budgets and the amount they are prepared to pay for each click.

It's an auction: advertisers are bidding for the keywords. Those who bid higher for a keyword will be displayed more frequently than those who bid lower. Lower bidding ads will only show when there are no higher bidding ads for that keyword or higher bidding ads have reached the limit of their daily or monthly budget. Obviously Google wants you to bid high for the keywords you want.

---

[121] https://www.google.com/accounts/ServiceLogin?service=adwords

[122] https://www.google.com/adsense

It's not as bad as it sounds. Within the limits you set, Google will only bid the minimum amount necessary for your ad to appear. If you bid 50c a click, but everyone else only bid 25c per click for your keywords, you'll pay 26c a click and maintain top position while you remain within budget.

With no monthly fee and just $5 to activate, Google Adwords get great reach with good control of your advertising budget. They are directly related to actions. Beyond getting the click, your website needs to be optimized to convert visitors to customers.

Getting the best from an Adwords campaign

The number of ad displays shown by Google is dependent on your daily budget, your maximum bid-per-click and your click-through rate. Yes, Google places ads that work (high click-through rate) ahead of ads that have very low click-through rates, because Google doesn't get paid until someone clicks. It's in their best interest to have ads that are getting clicked-on regularly display at a higher priority than those that people are ignoring. So here are some things you can do to get the best from your campaign.

Show your ad more

Your budget determines how many times the ad can be shown in a day. Your success rate compared to your bid rate will determine how much budget you allocated per day. When an ad is working you should improve the frequency.

If people are clicking through to your site from the ad, but not converting there, you need to be aware of that (from your Google Analytics package) and change the website to get better conversion rates for whatever action you're looking for from the ad.

Ads that get a lot of click-throughs will be displayed higher in the ad display block than those that don't.

Optimize your content and keyword targeting

You will already have data on what keywords people are searching for to find businesses like yours from your Analytics. They will be your starting point for the keywords you'll bid for with Adwords.

Make your ad compelling. Well, d'oh! Think like the potential customer and make it catch their attention, not yours or other industry insiders.

Keywords should not be too broad, or you'll get a lot of impressions (because the keywords match) but no results (because the ad isn't compelling). If the keywords are too narrowly focused you'll miss potential impressions and the chance to convert. Remember, Google likes ads that get clicks!

Google has a keyword suggestion tool[123] that will analyze your website, or descriptive phrase, and generate appropriate keywords. Use these as starting points and compare results using different keywords.

How should you write your ad?

Include your keywords in your ad text or title – keep it tightly associated with the keywords that will display the ad.

A simple clear style seems to work best.

Have a strong call to action. Encourage people to click to the next step.

Where should you link to?

Naturally you'll link to the most relevant page for each ads' potential customer. That will be a page that has been honed and optimized to convert the casual browser, having just clicked through from an Adword, into a customer.

Make sure the landing page is closely matched to the ad. People get very frustrated when they are misdirected in an attempt to hijack their attention. This will cost you your Adwords investment and not return value in sales.

Although Google tracks the click-through rate for each of the ads you place, you can also use tracking URLs for each ad or keyword. This will absolutely, clearly show you how many of your site visitors came from Google Adwords.

A tracking URL is appended to the end of the actual URL. For example:
http://www.proappstips.com/HDSurvivalHandbook/ will become http://www.proappstips.com/HDSurvivalHandbook/?referrer=source or
http://www.proappstips.com/HDSurvivalHandbook?referrer=source.

---

[123] https://adwords.google.com/select/KeywordToolExternal

The second version with the tracking URL should be used if testing the first version demonstrates inconsistent loading. Test each tracking URL in your browser before loading it to your Adsense ads.

These URLs will show in your Analytics files as coming from Google and you can simply count the entries where "Google" appears. (Analytics will also tell you what portion of your traffic comes from Google.)

Stay within Google's publishing guidelines

Google has quite specific editorial guidelines[124] for Adwords, but they can be summarized as:

* Clearly and accurately describe your site; and
* Emphasize the unique benefits of your production company's services over all others.

There is an extensive list of guidelines at Google covering:

Accurate Ad Text

Capitalization

Character Limits

Competitive Claims

Grammar & Spelling

Implied Affiliation

Inappropriate Language

Prices, Discounts, & Free Offers

Proper Names

Punctuation & Symbols

Repetition

Superlatives

Target Specific Keywords

Trademarks

Unacceptable Phrases

---

[124] http://adwords.google.com/support/bin/static.py?page=guidelines.cs&topic=9271&subtopic=9277

While losing access to Adwords isn't as devastating as transgressing Google's linking rules and having your site's pagerank (where it fits in Google's index of popularity) dropped, it isn't worth stepping outside the guidelines. At a minimum your ads are not going to run!

Adwords will only drive traffic to your website, from there it is up to you to convert the visitor to a customer at your site.

Google also maintains an extensive Help Center[125] for Adwords.

---

[125] http://adwords.google.com/support/

10: Cut Costs

One way to make more profit and grow your business is to cut costs. While personnel costs (and facility costs) will vary according to your business needs, there are a lot of ways to reduce costs without reducing quality of service.

Question the software you use: do you really need expensive proprietary software? I'm not giving up Final Cut Pro for Jahshaka[126] just yet (nor the many other open source editing alternatives[127], but I did stop using Adobe GoLive for my relatively simply HTML editing needs for SeaMonkey[128]. There are a lot of Open Source (free) software for business or web services for business to use.

Consider your officespace needs carefully. Of course, it will depend on the type of production business you have. If you're a full-featured post-production facility you'll need your own dedicated office space. If you're a producer or freelance editor, or like to work on your own system, you may not need full-time dedicated office space.

Other ways to reduce overhead and increase profitability are to reduce your hosting costs, review printing expenses and use free or inexpensive resources for stock footage or images, sound effects, textures, models, etc.

---

[126] http://jahshaka.org/

[127] http://en.wikipedia.org/wiki/
List_of_open_source_software_packages#Video_editing

[128] http://www.seamonkey-project.org/

Open Source or inexpensive Software

There is open source (free) or shareware[129]/inexpensive software options to replace most categories of commercial software.

Office

While the 'standard' is Microsoft Office, OpenOffice[130] has an excellent reputation, is available for all platforms and has very high compatibility with MS Office documents. For OS X users, NeoOffice[131] may be a better call as it's an OS X port of OpenOffice with a native look and feel.

While I have the Office suite purchased from Microsoft, I have found myself using Apple's Numbers over Excel (because it gives me greater layout and design control while being compatible with Excel documents) and Pages for all layout and publishing work. I continue to use Word primarily because I like starting with an outline and then convert that to a document by filling in the blanks under the outline. The latest version of Pages in iWork 09 includes this feature so when I upgrade I may have no need for MS Office at all. While not free at $79, iWork is substantially cheaper than MS Office.

Zoho[132] has mostly free online tools for documents and spreadsheets with the added advantage that multiple users can easily collaborate on the documents.

Google also have online document and spreadsheet tools[133] available free, with collaboration, as part of its offerings.

---

[129] Shareware software is freely distributed but the author expects a small payment if you use the software repeatedly. Usually there is some disincentive – like a nag screen or start-up delay – to not pay the fee and register.

[130] http://www.openoffice.org/

[131] http://www.neooffice.org/neojava/en/index.php

[132] http://www.zoho.com/

[133] The easiest way to find Google Docs log-in is to search for "Google Docs".

For accounting, scheduling and calendaring applications Mashable has an extensive list of more than 270 online solutions[134] you can access through a browser. Not all are free but most have a free option, even if it is more limited than their full service.

Presentations

There is a presentation module in OpenOffice but I prefer to use Keynote, part of the iWork suite. I have deleted Powerpoint from my hard drive completely.

Zoho Show is part of the Zoho suite of online tools. It might lack the more sophisticated features of Powerpoint or Keynote but it's hard to beat the price.

Google also have presentation tools as part of their office suite.

If none of those alternatives work for you, perhaps one of the 11 other alternatives Mashable rounded up in their collection of 13 online presentation tools[135] will work.

Collaborative presentations also mean you can, for some limited uses, replace WebEx for webinars, if the group is small.

Graphics and design

Adobe Photoshop is a power tool and I wouldn't want to work without it in my work. However, simpler tools exist. On Mac OS X Pixelmator[136] is built on OS X's Core Image technology. At US$59 it's not free, but compared with Photoshop, it's virtually free!

A free alternative for OS X is Paintbrush[137], which has an interface similar to MS Paint (Windows) or Apple's long lost MacPaint. Alternatively another open source project for OS X is Seashore[138], also built on core OS X technologies and Gimp.

---

[134] http://mashable.com/2008/09/21/270-online-business-tools/

[135] http://mashable.com/2008/02/16/forget-powerpoint-online-presentations/

[136] http://www.pixelmator.com/

[137] http://paintbrush.sourceforge.net/

[138] http://seashore.sourceforge.net/

Gimp[139] is the granddaddy of open source image editing programs. Gimp on OS X requires the extra hassle of installing Xwindows (a Unix GUI standard), but it is available for Windows.

Windows users might also consider Paint.net[140], Photoscape[141], Photoplus[142], Pixia[143], VCW VicMan's Photo Editor[144], or Ultimate Paint[145].

Online, Google have their free Picassa[146] software and online service. It's not a fully featured image editing program – more a photo manipulation and management tool like Apple's iPhoto. Like iPhoto, Picassa supports facial recognition across your library.

For 2D or 3D drawing and plans it's hard to beat Google Sketch Up[147].

For full-on 3D there's Blender[148] – one of the most popular open source 3D applications with a broad spectrum of modeling, texturing, lighting, animation and video post-processing functionality in one package. Through it's open architecture, Blender provides cross-platform interoperability, extensibility, a small footprint, and a tightly integrated workflow.

---

[139] http://www.gimp.org/

[140] http://www.getpaint.net/

[141] http://www.photoscape.org/ps/main/index.phpP

[142] http://www.freeserifsoftware.com/

[143] http://www.ne.jp/asahi/mighty/knight/

[144] http://www.vicman.net/vcwphoto/index.htm

[145] http://www.ultimatepaint.com/

[146] http://picasa.google.com/

[147] http://sketchup.google.com/

[148] http://www.blender.org/download/get-blender/

Web/Internet

Although Apple ship iWeb with all new Macs, it isn't a great tool for web design because the html it creates is not fully web standards compliant. That doesn't mean you need to go spend a fortune. As I noted above, I use SeaMonkey[149] for individual pages. It is available for OS X, Windows and Linux. SeaMonkey is not designed for site management, just individual pages.

If you're using Wordpress[150] for your blog, as I recommended, then you already have a simple CMS system. Current versions of Wordpress support static pages with very easy integration of graphic, audio and video elements. Thirty-one of the most useful plug-ins are listed in this article[151] by Andrew Lennon at The Daily Anchor. Listed are plug-ins for back-up, Search Engine Optimization, social media, video publishing, polls and more. With these plug-ins, plus the ability to make and index static pages, means Wordpress is well capable of even quite sophisticated web publishing.

For industrial-strength website building I strongly recommend Drupal[152] or Joomla[153]. These are ostensibly Content Management Systems, but because they are popular there are hundreds of extensions, plug-ins and additions that make it possible to build any modern website with dynamic content. Joomla is restricted to a single domain (excluding subdomains) per installation, whereas Drupal is more flexible. Drupal powers about 50 of the Warner Music band websites – one of the largest installations of this free software anywhere.

One of the best features is that there are many, many modules written for it, so that whatever function you need, there will be a module for Drupal already written and someone has written a tutorial on how to install and use it. Drupal's absolute best features

---

[149] http://www.seamonkey-project.org/

[150] http://wordpress.org/

[151] http://www.thedailyanchor.com/2009/03/23/31-wordpress-plugins-to-enhance-your-blog-and-life/

[152] http://drupal.org/

[153] http://www.joomla.org/

are that there is a lot of support material and that it is completely free, as in beer.

We have settled on Drupal for our future website development needs as it can easily integrate social networking modules for feeds and forums and dynamic pages. Currently our Intelligent Assistance main web store is running in Drupal. The various interface modules to our credit card processor and serial number management were all available as plug-ins.

Web encoding

While not totally free, Apple's QuickTime Player Pro is only US$29 and provides quick and easy encoding for web playback and Apple devices. The same encodes can be used in Flash players.

> **Note:** These days MPEG-4 movies (.mp4 or .m4v) with H.264 video and AAC audio are the industry standard. These files currently play in Flash Player 9, QuickTime Player and browser plug-in, Apple's iPods, iPhone and Apple TV. They will also play natively in Silverlight 3 due mid 2009 and the media player that will ship with Windows 7 in late 2009. Finally, there is one standard for online and downloadable video.

With a couple of free plug-ins QuickTime Player becomes a universal player, supporting just about every format available. You'll need Perian[154] and Telestream's free Windows Media components[155] for OS X. You can't play Windows Media with DRM with these on OS X (you can in some cases with Silverlight) but all other Windows Media plays back fine, and can be exported to editing codecs or industry standard MPEG-4. Anything QuickTime Player won't play with these add-on codecs will likely be playable in VLC[156]. (If neither will play the file, it's likely corrupt.)

---

[154] http://perian.org/
Note: Perian can conflict with some software, so note when you install it and if you get odd behaviors with Final Cut Studio then uninstall it.

[155] http://www.microsoft.com/windows/windowsmedia/player/wmcomponents.mspx

[156] http://www.videolan.org/vlc/

Other encoding or ripping tools are Handbrake[157] and FFmpeg[158]. FFmpeg is a cross-platform solution to record, convert and stream audio and video. Handbrake now uses the same decode library as FFmpeg and can use sources other than DVD as a result.

For a free alternative to Cinematize[159] or DVDxDV[160] for converting DVD source to editable video, MPEG Streamclip[161] works on both Mac and Windows and is free.

> **Note**: If you have source material on a DVD with copy protection, and you have the right to use that material granted by the copyright owner, then you can remove the copy protection with Mac the Ripper. Due to the provisions of the DMCA I'm not linking to the application but it can usually be found with a web search.

Project Management

Although not free, collaborative project management is available for a low monthly fee from 37 Signals through their Basecamp[162] web application.

Although free, dotproject.net[163] has not had development since 2003 and may not be fully supported.

Scripting and Pre-production

For script writing and pre-production, Celtx[164] is hard to beat. Celtx covers the entire pre-production process. Use it to write scripts (Final Draft compatible), prepare storyboards for scenes and sequence, develop your characters, breakdown and tag

---

[157] http://handbrake.fr/

[158] http://www.ffmpeg.org/

[159] http://www.miraizon.com/products/products.html

[160] http://www.dvdxdv.com/

[161] http://www.squared5.com/

[162] http://www.basecamphq.com/

[163] http://www.dotproject.net/

[164] http://www.celtx.com/

elements, schedule production and prepare production reports for cast and crew.

Celtx is a free, downloadable application for OS X, Windows and Linux.

Celtx Studio is an optional online service for collaboratively sharing the content created in Celtx. This service has a nominal annual charge per customer of US$50. (Customers with accounts can share and collaborate with their associates with the one account).

Editing, compositing and effects

While there are free editing, compositing and effects software available – do a Google search – I'm not yet prepared to recommend moving away from the mainstream commercial applications. The project that is furthest along and closest to commercial software is Jahshaka[165]. The Jahshaka team are building an open source, high end editing and compositing tool, but it remains a "work in progress" and is not yet ready for 'prime time'. Still, if you're growing in the business and not yet ready to invest in software, Jahshaka might be useful as a learning tool.

If you are not working on commercial projects, Apple, Adobe and Avid offer educational pricing on their mainstream editing tools. While you have to be a legitimate student (or teacher) to qualify, enrollment in a Community College course qualifies in most cases. It certainly is acceptable to Apple for Final Cut Studio purchases. These are not upgradable and not for commercial work, but are otherwise identical to their full-price versions.

---

[165] http://jahshaka.org/

Virtual Offices

Over the last 15 years our office needs have varied from over 21,000 square feet (about 2000 square meters) down to about 200 square feet right now. At the time we had that space we had a full postproduction facility and QuickTime authoring facility employing 9 people full time.

However, with digital sources and digital editing the equipment has become substantially smaller, quieter and cooler needing less space. In the last two years I've set up edit systems for specific movie projects that took as little as 200 square feet through to about 600 square feet. That latter space had two lounges, two workstations, equipment space and desks for producer and director.

The real savings come for producers and freelancers. Many of my clients have full commercial edit suites, producing work for Disney, Fox, Warner Bros and others, in dedicated space in their home. Apparently the stigma of working from home has passed.

Producers, writers and those whose office is not where the real work happens – a Director or DOP for example – truthfully don't need an office.

When we moved to the US and opened a US office we took a single room in a serviced office complex. We had only a small apartment and needed the extra space.

A serviced office was perfect. Our phones were answered for us, in our name and messages taken if we were out of the office. Packages would be received on our behalf if we weren't there. Because this was a small serviced office, with the owner the primary tenant, and not a serviced office/hot desk location in Beverly Hills (we were well into suburbia but on a main road) the cost was relatively inexpensive at under US$500 a month.

We also needed space for the DV Guys, and later Digital Production BuZZ, equipment. Later we moved to a smaller space in a shared building at nominal cost. Once we passed control of the BuZZ to a new owner, we found we had no real need for the space, other than an occasional meeting. We moved out of that space, retaining the address for official purposes, but moved into a larger apartment with a home office space, in an apartment complex that received packages on our behalf!

Meetings are either at client premises (saving them time) or we meet at a very nice coffee shop half a block away.

We're not the only ones with that idea because whenever we go to the coffee shop – for a meeting or just to work somewhere other than the apartment – it's always full of people writing or discussing a script. (We live in Burbank so that's not that surprising.)

Inexpensive rental premises can be found in older strip malls, particularly if they have an upstairs, a little off the beaten track.

Cheaper Hosting

If you're running a major web application you'll want the highest quality, highest availability hosting, but even that need not cost a fortune.

For a simple, mostly static promotional website with a business blog and demonstration pieces, 1and1.com[166] or Dreamhost.com[167] offer very inexpensive plans with generous storage and bandwidth options that they hope you'll never use! Still for less than $11 a month we host about a dozen low traffic domains for client sites and for my blog at philiphodgetts.com.

We also maintain an account on Media Temple's Gridserver, which is now quite stable on the newer Gridservers, because it can handle sudden spikes of traffic and database demand without crashing! You do pay for the extra services should that happen but that is much better than having the site crash or become unavailable because of sudden demand.

Even their dedicated virtual server – the equivalent of having your own server in a co-located facility – is only US$50 a month.

---

[166] http://1and1.com

[167] http://www.dreamhost.com/

High bandwidth media delivery

If you have to serve up a lot of video – more than a couple of Terabytes a month – then you should seriously consider Amazon's S3 service[168]. You would have to be serving 50-100 TB a month to get your distribution price down to the levels that Amazon charges for S3: 15c/GB per month for storage; 10c/GB for data transferred to your storage unit; and from 17c down to 10c/GB for outbound traffic, based on your needs.[169] These are the best rates for small-to-medium traffic since you cannot use a Dreamhost account for pure downloads. (It's a breach of their terms of service and yes, they do check!)

The best thing about Amazon's S3 is that you only pay for what you actually use, with no minimum costs per month. If you get a big increase in demand, it scales with you.

If you want to improve the delivery experience, then you can add their CloudFront[170] service for a simple Content Delivery Network. It's not Akami or Limelight but again there is no minimum commitment and no fees beyond what you use.

The only downside to the Amazon services is that they require a very small amount of programming expertise. Any competent web developer should set it up it within a couple of hours.

---

[168] http://aws.amazon.com/s3/

[169] Prices are subject to change by Amazon without notice and without automatically updating this book!

[170] http://aws.amazon.com/cloudfront/

Review printing costs

If you have been in the habit of simply renewing your print orders with a local printer, consider the savings to be made by going further away.

There are a number of people who will offer free business cards, with the caveat that their name and promotional line takes a small part of the reverse side. Vistaprint[171] and Overnight Prints[172] are two of the many printers offering free business cards. The other downside is that they have a limited range of designs so you might not get something exactly suitable for your business.

There are also places you should consider for full print orders. We have used Zoo Printing[173]. Even though they are based in the Los Angeles region we deal with them by uploading our artwork and having the printing delivered, often as little as 3 days later. The quality is acceptable, particularly for the price, but not for those who absolutely have to have the highest quality work.

Keep in mind that printing 50-100 pages of a promotional page using an inkjet printer will cost more for ink and paper than having four color printing done, such have the economics of printing changed over the last decade.

---

[171] http://www.vistaprint.com

[172] http://www.overnightprints.com

[173] http://www.zooprinting.com/

Use Free Resources

Believe it or not, there are lots of people who want to give you free textures, brushes, images, stock footage and royalty free music or sound effects.

Firstly, most people with Apple's Final Cut Studio forget that Soundtrack Pro not only comes with a large number of music loops, but also thousands of royalty free sound effects, many in 5.1 surround sound.

The best place to find free resources is via the Resource index[174] at the Digital Production BuZZ's BuZZdex. There you can search each type of resource – from contracts to stock footage – in 69 categories. (Not all indexed resources are free, but most are.)

There are free plug-ins for After Effects and Final Cut Pro, Templates, helpful applications and more. In the Stock category alone there are 11 sites offering free stock, including half a terabyte of public domain video, free for the downloading from Public.Resource.Org[175].

Also indexed are the NASA archive and other resources paid for by the US Government. Listed in the BuZZdex of resources is a list made by Rich Harrington's Photoshop for Video[176] site that itself lists 17 US Government sites with free photos or video.

> Technically they're only free to US citizens or residents, as the US Taxpayers paid for these resources to be created, but few restrictions are placed on use overseas.

Search Flickr[177] for photos. What you need to know is that photographs uploaded to Flickr carry many different copyright restrictions. Anything marked "All Rights Reserved" are covered by traditional copyright restrictions – i.e. you can't use them without explicit permission from the copyright own.

---

[174] http://www.digitalproductionbuzz.com/BuZZdex/resources/

[175] http://bulk.resource.org/ntis.gov/

[176] http://photoshopforvideo.com/resources/free/free.html

[177] http://www.flickr.com/

Say I'm looking for an image of the Hollywood sign. After a couple of false starts I find this image[178]. Instead of "All Rights Reserved" this image is covered by a Creative Commons[179] (CC) license. In this specific instance, if I used the image I would need to provide a caption with attribution to the creator, the work I create cannot be for commercial purposes and any derivative works must have the same type of CC license.

However, searching a little further I found this image[180] of the sign with a more generous CC license: "If you use this photo, please list the photo credit as "Scott Beale / Laughing Squid" and link the credit to laughingsquid.com." That is what I have done.

---

[178] http://www.flickr.com/photos/vlastula/450642954/sizes/l/

[179] http://en.wikipedia.org/wiki/
Creative_commons#Types_of_Creative_Commons_Licenses

[180] http://www.flickr.com/photos/laughingsquid/271688397/

11: Work smarter

Once you have all this increased business, you'll need to work smarter to fit it all in! Working smarter, also known as improving your productivity, benefits a businessperson at every level.

If you can get things done faster, or cheaper, it's the same as making more time or money. People should make more use of the Internet to find the answers to business or technical questions.

With modern technologies there are ways to produce less expensively while maintaining quality, certainly in postproduction where expensive Storage Area Networks (SAN) are giving way to inexpensive Ethernet-based SANs.

There's always the option to outsource some work to less expensive providers, as the animation industry has been doing for years by having animation created offshore.

It doesn't hurt to get paid faster for the work you do. It saves running an expensive overdraft and it improves your overall cash position. Profit is great, but if you run out of cash waiting to collect then you're out of business, while making a profit.

Search the Internet

I'm much smarter by email than in person because I can always do a quick search of the Internet before responding. This is either because I need to check a detail that I'm uncertain of, or because I have no idea but assume the answer "is out there." It almost always is, if you know how to search properly. It appears to me that most people do not think to search or don't know how to most effectively search.

I really only use Google as my search engine, however there are others I use for specific purposes. Pipl.com[181] for people searches – it finds information that doesn't come up in Google – and Clusty.com[182], which searches across multiple search engines and groups (clusters) the results by general topic.

---

[181] http://pipl.com

[182] http://clusty.com/

Add extra search terms

Yesterday I wanted to know if QuickTime supported Byte Range requests.[183] Searching on "QuickTime" gave only a little over 33 million results, with my needle of knowledge lost in that haystack of results. Search on "QuickTime byte range request" dropped the number of responses to a little over 4,000, with useful results in the first page. (It does but your server has to be set up for it.)

Search one website

Recently I was looking for a page at the Academy of Television Arts and Sciences so I started with [Next TV Academy Television Arts]. Not so useful. Since I knew the page I was looking for was at the emmys.org website, the next search was [Next TV site:emmys.org] and it was found.

Use Quotes

By default search engines will bring back a result where all the search terms are present on a page, even if they're not together. This is not so useful for names. For example if I search on [Open TV Network] (without inverted commas) the first two main hits are relevant, but the third result is 'Open Student TV Network'. To get only the results that exactly match Open TV Network search with the search terms in quote marks, so it looks exactly like ["Open TV Network"]. With the exact match, the number of results drops from around 63 million pages that contain all three words 'open', 'tv' and 'network ' down to the 1030 that are talking about my company. This is far more useful than the original result.

If you're getting too many irrelevant results, even with additional keywords, use the quote marks for exact matches on two or more words. You can have a mixture. To continue our example if I wanted to find those pages that had the lead developer's name and Open TV Network together I would search for ["Open TV Network" "Greg Clarke"] and I get two instances of the same post on my personal blog. Changing the search term to ["Open TV

---

[183] A Byte Range request is used for http downloadable video to search ahead, forcing the download to "start over" but from a point later in the video, simulating random access. The difference between the start and the requested starting point is the byte range. You can see this demonstrated in Flash on YouTube.

Network" "Gregory Clarke"] there is only one result – a post on the Avid-L (a Yahoo email group for editors working with Avid).

Another recent example: I was trying to find the keys to press for the open bullet character. My initial search was [open bullet character in OS X]. Because that was way too many irrelevant results, I tried again with ["open bullet" character "OS X"] to get closer to useful results.

Try quote marks around a unique phrase or sentence you've written in an article or interview, and you'll discover whether or not it's been quoted or plagiarized.

Phrase for the answer instead of the question

Most pages that have answers do not necessarily also repeat the question. I've found it much more satisfying to think of how the answer might be phrased and enter that instead.

For example, instead of [What is the average life of an Anton-Bauer battery], where I find there are a lot of other people asking the same question, but no obvious page with an answer, [Anton-Bauer battery lasts recharge cycles] got me much closer. Combining this tip with the increased number of search terms led me to [Anton-Bauer battery lasts recharge cycles professional video camera] and therefore to the answer.

Exclude misleading terms

Words that have multiple meanings are particularly problematic in searches. If I were looking for video editors and my initial search on ["video editor"] bought in around 5 million results (even with the quote marks – over 100 million without them). Looking at the results I get, I see there's confusion between video editor – the person – and video editor – the software. So exclude any page with software on it from the search by using ["video editor" – software -program].

A classic non-industry example is a search on [meatloaf]. Since I'm actually looking for a recipe [meatloaf –music – album] is a whole lot more palatable than Mr Aday would be.

Leave out the "stop" words

The so-called "stop" words are simply those words that Google (and most search engines) will ignore because they are so common in the language that they are not indexed. These would be words like:

> "the, on, where, how, de, la, as well as certain single digits and single letters".

Learn about businesses

Entering a company name, suburb and zip code will bring up a direct link to any matching web page, a map and phone number.

Enter a street address in the Google search, or in maps.google.com and the businesses at that address will be listed (although it's not perfect).

Look up phone numbers and addresses

To find the geographic coverage of a telephone area code, search for [818 area code] and you'll be offered a map of that area code.

To look up the business behind a phone number simply type the number in. Try it in all formats: 8182062415 does not bring up the company information but would allow you to find it via one of our sites; 818-206-2415 brings up our main website at IntelligentAssistance.com; 818 206 2415 gives the same result as with the dashes because Google considers a dash to be the same as a space. (It does not consider and underscore _ as a space).

Track Packages

Enter the digits from a FedEx or UPS package number and Google will offer a link to the tracking information. Sure you can do that by first going to the website but if you've got to type the number in – instead of following a link in an email – you can get there faster by using Google.

Calculator and converter

OK it's not a scientific calculator but you can perform reasonably complex math by simply typing the equation into the Google search box. Type in (60*60*24*30) to find the average number of seconds in a month.[184]

Type in [72 degrees Fahrenheit in Celsius] and Google will respond with 22.2222 etc degrees Celsius. This works for most units of measure: [meters in 10 foot] gives the expected answer, for example.

Definitions

Get definitions of words from all over the web by entering [define:supercalifragilisticexpialidocious] in the regular search box. (Yes, there are results.)

Watch your stock

Type in the ticker identifier for the stock – AAPL or MSFT and Google will return the current Apple or Microsoft stock price, graphs, financial news and so on. (Because there is no differentiation between Avid's corporate name and the stock ticker, this doesn't work for that company).

Product or ISBN code

Google is a bar code scanner! Type in the Universal Product Code (UPC) number, such as 735854234065 and Google will offer the product description as one of the high-ranking links.

Track flights

Type in the airline and flight number – United 840, for example – and the top link will be the current flight status for that flight.

If you're a real aviation buff, type in the aircraft registration number (on the tail) and see the full registration form for that plane, although I haven't been able to test his personally.

---

[184] Months vary from 28 to 31 days. This calculator assumes 30 days, but for any specific month you want to calculate, use the actual number of days in the month if it varies from 30.

Identify cars from their VIN number

Type in the Vehicle Identification Number (VIN) and Google will return the car's year, make and model. I'm not sure how useful this might be as the VIN number is etched into a plate on the door frame (or just below the windscreen). If you can read it, you can probably tell the make and model of the car you're standing next to! (If you have the VIN number from a registration form, then it could be useful).

Image Search

As well as the occasional vanity search, for pictures of myself other people may have taken and put online somewhere, Google Images[185] is a great place to search for logos and product shots, or even places and people.

Google allows you to search for all sizes or specify Extra Large, Large, Medium or Small images. (Personally I'd prefer a way to choose Large or Extra Large to avoid having to do the search twice, but this is the way it is right now.)

Most of the search secrets above also apply to Google Images – more words, quotation marks, excluded words – to make the search results more useful.

Google is not doing a full image search – no facial recognition here! It uses the associated text on the page and any caption or alt tag on the image, which can lead to some odd images being discovered. That is why it's important to put titles and captions on images.

I discovered while researching this section, that Google Images now also includes videos that match the search terms!

> **Important:** Unlike stock photography or Flickr, Google provides no information on the copyright status of any image. I generally consider using a product shot when talking about a camera or deck, or using a company logo in a review to be fair use. Beyond that, be careful to do the right thing. Fortunately the image is shown in context, which usually provides a way to contact the website owner at least.

---

[185] http://images.google.com

How to Produce More Cheaply

Although this is likely to be the most controversial section of the book, it's also probably the one you are most likely to use the most.

All types of production are undergoing downward budgetary pressure. Some of this is simply equipment driven and of the industry's own causing. For many years production and postproduction facilities pointed to the standard of equipment they used (or format) to indicate that they were "professional". Then one day that equipment went up in quality and way, way down in price. Clients who understood they were paying for access to expensive equipment suddenly questioned the cost of production when the equipment went down so far in price.

Smart companies saw this coming and long ago stopped talking about the equipment and tools of production as their differentiating factor and moved to promoting their skills and talent at communication. (See the earlier section on Clarifying you Brand).

What the drop in production costs has created is the ability to create a program in almost every budget arena. How can we do that? We do that by adopting changes in technology and business that favor lower budget production without cheapening the look.

How much you are able to take advantage of these cost reductions depends entirely on the type of work you do and how technically pure your clients need you to be. Keep in mind that even Discovery now accepts HDV as source for their "Bronze" programs (and smaller amounts in higher tiers of programming).

Here are my Top 10 tips for producing cheaper. Pass on the cost savings to keep clients coming back for more; or hold onto the savings and make more profit.

I Don't pay for quality your clients won't see.

This is the number one recommendation and one that's sure to be controversial. A number of my friends are very quality focused: for them uncompressed 10 bit is a compromise on native film quality! (Ok, I exaggerate a little, but you know what I mean.) These people eschew "consumer" formats (like HDV and AVCHD/AVCAM) because they don't meet their quality expectations.

Quality is fine. I've got no problem with shooting on Viper cameras, and conforming the offline edit to the 4:4:4 source for the Digital Intermediate if you're heading for major film distribution. There will always be work that requires the highest quality, but that is not the majority of independent production.

If your client won't see the difference between something shot with a 3-chip camera and a Thompson Viper, why spend the extra on the camera rental and the digital lab work to process to something editable? If it doesn't add value on the screen for your client, don't spend it.

Over the last two years I've advised on a number of projects where compressed workflows were indistinguishable from uncompressed workflows. The first example was a multicam Saturday morning show being edited from the switched studio shoot, and the individual cameras. The company was "offlining" this SD project with DVCPRO 50 and then onlining to 10 bit uncompressed from Digital Betacam source. The uprez was taking them 18 hours a show and causing enormous issues for the Assistant Editors.

I suggested that they finish in DVCPRO 50 as it was a perfect match for the Digital Betacam source and challenged them to point to any visible difference between the DVCPRO 50 and uncompressed 10 bit. When nobody – from the Post Production Supervisor down to the editors and assistants – could see the difference, the decision was made to use the DVCPRO 50 versions to finish.[186]

---

[186] DVCPRO 50, like DV, is 480 lines only, so there are an additional 6 lines of blanking. Extended blanking is no longer likely to get a show rejected for QC reasons. In this instance, the company was already expanding the images slightly in the online bay to eliminate some side blanking from the source, which also hid the missing six lines in DVCPRO 50 compared with full raster SD NTSC at 486.

A film project – going direct to DVD as the third in a movie franchise – was edited in ProRes 422 HQ upon my recommendation. HDCAM dailies were captured direct to ProRes 422. The color correction and DVD Mastering all used those ProRes 422 files, greatly, simplifying the workflow.

On another film project – the fifth in a popular franchise – was shot with a Thompson Viper and the digital lab converted the Viper images to editable ProRes 422 HQ. The producer asked for the "highest quality" 'offline' in case he could persuade the director to not do a 4:4:4 conform. Given that the release was DVD only, and the market for this franchise would not perceive any difference, the company ultimately saved the $70,000 that a conform of the Viper source would have cost, by doing color correction of the ProRes 422 (HQ) footage.

In both the last two examples, the 'film' was only going to be seen on DVD and the audience was the established audience for the franchise.

Once we get beyond a certain quality threshold (different for every targeted audience) there is no added value in producing in ever-higher, ever-more-expensive workflows "because we can, and we care about quality." Clients and audiences only care about the "good enough" quality. If you doubt me, go visit 10 of your non-industry friends and see how well adjusted their home TV sets are.

You could rent a Viper or Sony F23 for a film project or buy a RED One digital cinema camera for the project. The audience, even for a project distributed on film, won't see the marginal quality improvement that the extra cost of the Viper/F23 theoretically provides.

Will an event client see the difference between a decent HDV camera and a $40,000 Panasonic or Sony camera? Does their home display come close to showing either source to maximum benefit?

Will a corporate client see, let alone worry about, so-called rolling shutter issues with an EX-1?

Don't sweat the formats and gear. Even the cheapest modern HD camcorders aimed at the consumer market deliver "to die for" quality of just a few years back.

Compression is your friend

Compressed formats like DVCPRO 50; ProRes 422 and Avid's DNxHD codecs are your friend. ProRes and DNxHD both do HD work, with minimal compression, at Standard Definition data rates.

This brings great benefit: lower storage costs and easy SAN (Storage Area Network) configurations. Not only is there less storage required (usually less than ¼ that of uncompressed 10 bit) but the storage does not have to be as fast, because the data rates are lower.

These high-quality, compressed formats make it possible to design a SAN based on Gigabit Ethernet[187], instead of requiring expensive Fiber Channel.

2   Put the money where it gives the best payback

If it's not worth spending more than the client will perceive on the gear, it is worth spending money on decent lighting and sound. Lighting makes the pictures look great: far more so than any format change.

Research has shown that high quality audio is the cheapest way to "improve the perceived image quality". Apparently good audio makes audiences think the pictures look better than the same pictures with poor-to-average audio.

Lighting

Gain some expertise in creative lighting then build a basic kit in whichever technology you prefer, although these days I'd be considering LED and fluorescent lighting over more traditional incandescent sources. LED and fluorescent lighting are low heat, which saves on air-conditioning needs (or prevents uncomfortably hot location shoots). LED lighting units, in particular, are smaller and lighter to transport.

Remember, with modern cameras, control of light is more important than the gross amount, once you clear the minimum exposure level that will keep the camera from deteriorating into noise.

---

[187] http://magazine.creativecow.net/article/build-your-own-affordable-san-that-iworksi

Create some basic configurations you know well, and – along with your team – you can assemble quickly for the majority of the work you do. Creative flexibility and experimentation are for higher budget opportunities.

My ideal kit would be a LitePanel 1x1[188], Two Lightpanel mini's[189] and Lightpanel Micro[190] for a camera light. That kit will come to US$3880 and is highly recommended. If you look inside the back pages of the trade magazines you'll find less expensive competitive offerings. One of the nice things about LED is that they can be dimmed without changing color temperature. If you're still looking for alternatives check out Zylight[191].

Audio

Quality audio takes much more effort than using the built-in camera microphone, but that isn't news to anyone, I'm sure. Invest in some good quality (Sennheiser or Lectrosonics) radio microphone systems and mini-shotgun system if you can, but for a budget kit here are my recommendations. (The higher price of the Sennheiser or Lectrosonics systems is offset by robustness of the gear, particularly the Lectrosonics microphones. That will mean they last many more years than cheaper gear, and you'll have the reassurance that "it just works".)

Boom microphones can be expensive and, in general, you pay for what you get. The top-end Sennheiser[192] shotgun will run you around $2500 – way over the top for a budget kit. Instead I would settle on an Azden SGM-1X[193] – Super-Cardioid Shotgun Condenser Microphone at $150. It's a good compromise that can be used on camera for directional atmosphere or on a pole for talent audio. You'll need a windshield and the K-ZFC Slip-On

---

[188] http://www.s131567196.onlinehome.us/products/onebyone.asp

[189] http://www.s131567196.onlinehome.us/products/minisystem.asp

[190] http://www.s131567196.onlinehome.us/products/micro.asp

[191] http://www.zylight.com/servlet/StoreFront

[192] http://www.sennheiser.com/sennheiser/home_en.nsf

[193] http://www.azdencorp.com/shop/customer/product.php?productid=93298

Fleecy Windscreen[194] (Long) from K-Tek will do the job for around $80.

That boom pole you'll be needing, along with some strong arms to hold it for any length of time, also comes from K-Tek[195]. If there was the budget available I'd go for one of theirs.

If I had the budget I'd go for the K-Tek KA-113CCR 6-Section Articulated Boom Pole[196] with XLR Coiled Cable (Side Exit) and 5 Locking Positions – Measuring 1.4 to 9.5' for around $800, but instead we'll go for the K-Tek KEG-88 Traveler Carbon Fiber Boom Pole[197] at $370. (Yes, I know that's more than the microphone, but the pole will continue to do duty long after you upgrade the microphone.)

Like shotguns, radio microphones come in a wide range of prices. Highly desirable is a diversity receiver[198]. In diversity receivers there are two independent receivers, with their own aerials, and the receiver chooses whichever output has the best signal, moment by moment. I'm going for a Samson Concert[77] – Wireless Lavalier Microphone System with CR77 Receiver, CT7 Body-Pack Transmitter with Samson LM5 Lavalier Microphone at $220, which is the lowest price diversity system at B&H photo.

You'll also need (or someone will) noise isolating headphones for location monitoring. Figure at least $50 and up. Budget $100 for cables and audio adapters for getting direct feeds from mixers and PA systems.

---

[194] http://www.bhphotovideo.com/c/product/515498-REG/ K_Tek_K_ZFC_L_K_ZFC_Slip_On_Fleecy_Windscreen.html

[195] http://www.ktekbooms.com/

[196] http://www.ktekbooms.com/products.php?id=39

[197] http://www.ktekbooms.com/products.php?id=73

[198] http://www.jamminpower.com/main/diversity.jsp

3 Maximize the value of your hardware and software

Whenever there are new versions of software or new hardware for our various NLE solutions, it's tempting to run out and buy, but lock up those lease approvals and cut the credit card: you do not need the latest and the greatest.

Hardware and software continue to do the things they were doing when you purchased them – probably the software improved a bit with some free updates during the 'current release' period.

> *Unless your business has changed, and your customers' demands have increased, there's no reason to upgrade. Heresy!*

Unless you've moved to RED or work with AVCHD/AVCAM, Final Cut Pro 5.1 (or 4.5) will still be a useful creative tool and make you a lot of money. (Ditto for Media Composer 2.7. Heck even OS 9 Meridien Avids are still in everyday use cutting movies in 'Hollywood'.)

Again, if your clients don't perceive the value, and it's not going to make you significantly more productive, skip an update. I have one client working on major studio DVD extras, among other work, with a Final Cut Pro 4.5 Cinewave system. It's doing the job and he's making money with it long after it's been paid off.

> **Important Note:** If you are working with an older version of an NLE, *never* upgrade your Operating System or QuickTime version beyond those recommended for that software version. Ignore this advice and you will see instability, crashing or things "just not working."

Hardware

There are two schools of thought with hardware: work it until it's dead – 3-5 years – or replace it and sell the old while it still has value – every 2 years.

We're in a particularly odd place right now with Apple transitioning to all-Intel and increasingly software will only run on the newer hardware. (Snow Leopard – Mac OS X 10.6 – is expected to only run on Intel.) This is really reducing the value of PPC hardware, suggesting if you've got PPC hardware sell it now, or keep using it in less demanding functions indefinitely.

Personally, I consider turning over computer hardware every two years the better strategy. A two-year-old Mac has resale value, which reduces the "change-over" cost. Two year old Macs are now Intel: the last PPC Mac will be three years old when Snow Leopard ships.

Windows hardware can be upgraded progressively, if you're the tinkering type. Otherwise, I'd also suggest a 2-3 year cycle. If you plan on upgrading your Windows operating system version, plan on a new PC to accommodate it. (Windows 7 may be the exception to this advice. We will wait and see.)

Right now might be a good time to stretch out your Windows PC purchase until 64 bit systems become more affordable. Both platforms are moving toward 64 bit support to address larger amounts of memory in applications and to boost performance. Of the major NLE companies only Premiere Pro CS4 takes advantage of 64 bit processing (on Windows only). Avid and Apple have significant work to do to create 64 bit versions of their applications and those are not expected for at least another two years.

4   Stay away from bleeding edge technology (unless there's a huge payoff).

In front of the leading edge is the bleeding edge, where the pioneers are those with arrows in their back pointing the way for the settlers that follow. Avoid the bleeding edge, unless there's a huge payback in jumping on new technology early.

One example of where jumping early has made sense for many people is RED One – the first digital cinema camera from RED Digital Cinema. While I'm not a digital cinema producer, I can see the cost saving compared to renting more expensive (and traditional) high end electronic cinematography cameras being appealing enough to compensate for the 'bleeding edge' workflows.

The bleeding edge affects productivity. Things don't go according to plan and unexpected problems arise. Likewise, conventional wisdom is to not buy "version 1" of anything as the bugs are probably not fully tested in the real world. It's always wise to wait a little on new software releases to learn from your braver brethren whether there are unforeseen complications from the release.

So don't be the first to install that new version of QuickTime, or the new OS update. Hold back – patience grasshopper – and wait a couple of weeks. You'll remain productive on the system you're making money with until it's safe to upgrade.[199]

If you are going to adopt something unproven, like new production technology, a new version of the OS, or a new format, test, test and test some more before committing. Rent a camera if you don't own one (or borrow if you can) and shoot some footage. Capture it, do a simple edit, color correct – if color correction will be part of your postproduction – and output the file to the destination format. When it all works in your testing, you're then ready to start production.

5   Learn from Guerilla Filmmakers

Stu Mashwitz posted a lot of great tips on how independent producers can add extra production value to their projects by having a video camera with them at all times. In The DV Rebel's Guide[200], Stu tells of how he used a Fire Engine call-out to his neighborhood to capture shots of ladder trucks and the like, and firemen moving around, as production shots for a show featuring a fire in a nearby apartment.

That's just one example of how you can capture footage of stuff that's happening around you to add value you could never afford to your project. Stu avoided the costs of closing the street and calling out a Fire Truck, which he could never afford, to add many thousands of dollars worth of value.

NBC's *Friday Night Lights* is produced in a professional version of the guerilla style. Each scene is shot on location with multiple cameras in a documentary style shoot. Rehearsal is kept to a minimum so the blocking looks real. This not only lends a semi-documentary feel to the show, but it also makes production very much faster. At a TV Academy "Evening with Friday Night Lights" the cast said that they were often finished the days allocated script pages by mid afternoon, something

---

[199] The single exception is where an upgrade offers a solution to a problem you have been experiencing. Then the potential benefit outweighs possible problems.

[200] http://www.amazon.com/gp/product/0321413644

almost unheard of in TV production. *Friday Night Lights* costs 1/3 less per show than most dramas

At a similar evening for *Mad Men*, writer/producer Matthew Weiner said that television production was going to have to adopt an "Independent film model of television production" based on the techniques adopted by independent filmmakers. (He also said to "get used to not getting a 15 share" but making a decent profit.)

Design for cheap production

It's unlikely you're going to produce a *Battlestar Galactica* on a shoestring budget, but the final season of *Star Trek Enterprise* dropped the budget over half a million dollars an episode in an attempt to keep the show in production.

When you're budget constrained, develop the project appropriately. Joss Whedon's *Dr Horrible's Singalong Blog*[201] is 45 minutes of high quality musical comedy television production for about $400,000, under a SAG low budget contract. This is dramatically lower than regular network show budgets of $1-2 million for a similar show. There were relatively few sets and those were mostly "close in" action. The project was designed for high quality but with a low budget.

6   Go for the B talent

NBC/Fox's Hulu went for great talent for their 2009 Superbowl ad – NBC's own star Alec Baldwin, star of *30 Rock*. While Hulu can justify that expense, star power does very little for independent projects, particularly projects in corporate, education or event production.

Actors, generally, like their craft and they like to perform. That's why Los Angeles is dotted with "99 seat theaters" – small performance spaces where actors get only nominal payments for performances (and generally nothing for rehearsal). Similarly there is acting talent in every town.

In my former production life in Newcastle, Australia, I tapped into the local pool of "amateur" acting talent (with a sprinkling of 2 or 3 people attempting to act professionally) for a series of programs I made that were dramatic pieces. We were able to produce some very high-value pieces without breaking the client's budget. using

---

[201] http://drhorrible.com/

up to 20 actors (including extras) in one show with about 8-10 speaking parts.

There are over 120,000 (mostly unemployed) actors in the Screen Actors Guild. There are many, many more actors around the country and the world. Almost everywhere you can find great talent who, because they're not trying to make a living, are great value to the independent producer.

The same goes for voice-over talent. Every regional or local radio station has talent. If your budget is really, really constrained consider a college radio station for your talent.

Similarly, a top notch, Guild-certified editor brings many years experience to the job, but may not bring that much value to your corporate video or trade-show piece. You can find beginner talent at every film school and film/video department in any University.

You'll want to avoid the total beginners, except as Interns, and look for the pool of experienced talent that exists for every editing platform. You need someone competent and creative for education, corporate or hobby-interest video; not someone who's most recent experience earned them an Oscar or Emmy nomination!

With 1.25 million seats of Final Cut Pro sold (and probably that may again pirated) there are many, many, many competent editors who are interested in a decent living doing what they love doing: editing.

7   Step out of the mainstream for locations

You're not going to shoot on Hollywood Blvd, at the Griffith Observatory, in Times Square or on any major freeway without paying for the privilege.

When Bruce Branit and Jeremy Hunt wanted to make a short film of a big commercial aircraft making an emergency landing on the 405 Freeway, they didn't stop traffic for the shoot. Instead they shot extended takes of traffic on the freeway. They sliced segments of the shoot – where there were no cars as they moved through the shot – to make a single clean background plate they could animate into. They repeated this process for every angle they used for the short movie. 405 The Movie[202] had visual effects equal to the best Hollywood blockbuster and a budget that wouldn't cover one lunch for the crew for that blockbuster.

Digital stills as plates, along with well-lit green screen, can substitute for many locations. Green screen (or blue screen for film work) does not have to be limited to the studio. Rigging enough green fabric around the action area to isolate the actor can make them appear much closer in than the real location. Shoot on practical locations where the foreground is similar and key in the real background from a digital still.

A grass area and a green screen for the foreground and digital stills taken during a trip to the Griffith Observatory can save thousands of dollars in location fees, as an example. Shoot outdoors to get matching lighting without too much hassle.

Unless you have to do major lighting, street shoots can often be done without formal permission because you're done and wrapped before anyone can complain.

> **Tip:** Forgiveness is always easier to get than permission.

Avoid the sidewalk near, and foyers of, major office buildings and inside malls. They have security guards who frequently hassle videographers and photographers. The inside of buildings and malls are private property. Exteriors, in most cases, are easy to shoot and cut in shots from another location that have been chosen to match, or with some effort cement the foreground and a matching digital still. (Motion track foreground and background for hand-held production.)

Don't forget that not all productions need "real" locations. I did a number of productions in simple black spaces where minimal furniture and lighting (along with a great sound track) created the illusion of sets. These pieces were designed to not need realistic sets. The savings let us spend higher production values, like renting a crane for more interesting angles and quicker setups within that space.

---

[202] http://www.405themovie.com/

The space, as it turns out, was underutilized areas of our business property. Total cost for locations (above or regular rent) – about 4 gallons of flat black paint.

If producing for a client, suggest the client organize locations "to keep costs down." Just make sure the locations are practical for production!

An extreme case of what can be done when creative minds get to work against limited resources, is the work done on *Star Wreck: In the Perkinning*[203] produced – according to an interview I did with its creators Samuli Torssonen and Timo Vuorensola on the Digital Production BuZZ in 2006 – in a 12' x 10' room with a green screen. Actors mostly didn't work together, delivering individual performances that were later composited into the digital sets. The whole piece, available for free download from the link above, is well worth watching to see what can be done with limited budget and enough time. The 3D animation is studio grade. (The production is the most-watched Finnish movie of all time.)

8   Use Templates as starting points

In the Apple universe, Motion comes with a substantial number of Templates; LiveType even more so (and many backgrounds and animated elements that can be used in other applications by embedding them in a LiveType project).

In Avid's universe, Marquee comes with an enormous number of titling presets. Avid 3D ships with many stock 3D scenes and objects, along with 3D titling animation presets, while Avid FX (a.k.a. Boris RED) also ships with hundreds of presets and animations already complete and ready for your footage.

Adobe ship many titling animation presets with After Effects.

Yes, using Motion Templates (known as Master Templates in Final Cut Pro) means your work isn't completely unique: from time-to-time you'll see the template used elsewhere, but they save an enormous amount of time.

Not only are there the templates supplied by Apple for Motion/ Final Cut Pro, there are many third-party vendors:

---

[203] http://www.starwreck.com/

- Mark Spencer (who wrote the official Apple Pro Training guide for Motion) has teamed with Ripple Training[204] to create Motion Templates;

- Motion VFX[205] have an enormous number of SD and HD Motion Templates for individual purchase, along with After Effects presets as well.

- Motion Templates Online[206] have a deal where you 'buy one, get four free' Motion Templates.

- DVCreators.net[207] and DigMo![208] Both have free templates for download.

- LME produce After Effects projects as presets[209], similar to Motion Templates but for Adobe's compositing application.

Even commercial templates will save considerable money compared with designing your own, similarly complex, compositions from scratch. They, along with LME's After Effect project presets, can be completely customized and resaved as a new Master Template for use in Final Cut Pro or to share among all editors on a project.

9   Go "cheap" on stock, 3D models and music

Television special effects are, almost by definition, budget constrained compared with their film cousins. Such that, according to an article at Post[210] magazine, Master Key[211], buy in 3D

---

[204] http://www.applemotion.net/page21/page21.html

[205] http://www.motionvfx.com/

[206] http://motiontemplatesonline.com/

[207] http://www.dvcreators.net/free-motion-templates-and-resources/

[208] http://www.digmo.co.uk/software/free-apple-motion-templates/

[209] http://toolfarm.stores.yahoo.net/lme.html

[210] http://www.postmagazine.com/ME2/dirmod.asp?sid=&nm=&type=Publishing&mod=Publications%3A%3AArticle&mid=8F3A7027421841978F18BE895F87F791&tier=4&id=1BBF32EA9D254A74925E85D35560B7C4

[211] http://www.mkvfx.com

models from <u>TurboSquid</u>[212] or <u>3D Export</u>[213] for the new *Knight Rider* TV series.

It is substantially cheaper to buy a model than to model an object from scratch. If you look, there are also free 3D models on the Internet.

Likewise there are a lot of free sound effects available but the sites are generally hard to navigate and often filled with advertising. For professional quality sound effects that you can actually find on the site, <u>Sound Dogs</u>[214] has the "brand" recognition. With sound effects from $2.50 to $5.00 instantly downloadable, it's hard to go past it. Not to forget that, if you use Final Cut Studio, Apple includes a very extensive sound effects and sound design elements library with Soundtrack Pro. In stereo or 5.1 surround, these elements, along with the music loops also included, are royalty free for your productions.

Although you won't immediately think of them, <u>iStockPhoto</u>[215] now carry a wide range of sound effects, moving picture stock and still image stock, all at very reasonable prices, particularly if you compare the stock photos with more traditional suppliers like Getty Images: $1 – $21 dollars per image instead of hundreds of dollars per image. Video stock varies from $15 (web video size) to around $90 for HD video per clip.

10   Use smart software tools to save time and therefore money

When Avid released Media Composer V1 it was an advance look at what was to come, because by itself it was unimpressive, with a 160 x 120 4 bit (16 gray) "video monitor", where it was hard to see whether a mouth was open or closed!

Similarly, 20 years later we are moving into an era where software workflow tools can start to take out some of the repetitive chores and let smart producers and editors work much faster than their

---

[212] http://www.turbosquid.com/

[213] http://www.3dexport.com/

[214] http://sounddogs.com/

[215] http://www.istockphoto.com

competitors. Faster equals cheaper with lower costs to clients or higher profit for the producer.

Assisted Editing from Intelligent Assistance[216]

Obviously I would propose the software tools I've been involved in creating as part of the new smart toolkit. First Cuts for FCP automates the process of creating the first rough edits of a long form documentary. Feed it your log notes and First Cuts will send back to Final Cut Pro a technically competent edit to use as a starting point, or simply to explore the stories present in the material as stories, not as individual clips.

The companion software to First Cuts is Finisher for FCP. Finisher takes an A-roll (audio/radio cut) and adds lower third titles and b-roll. Finisher works with all the log notes created for Finisher, or for simple edits, simply the names of the clips are enough.

Our third product, Sync-N-Link for FCP not only automates the process of synchronizing dual system sound using matching time of day Timecode (TOD) ahead of editorial, but it can replace the camera audio from the edit at the end of editorial.

XMiL Workflow Tools[217]

XMiL Placer is for people who work on visual effects-heavy shows, who have to put a lot of iterations of visual effects shots into the cut on an ongoing basis.

XMiL Exporter works on clips contained in a XML export from Final Cut Pro. It generates text files for import into database applications. Those text files can also contain information on markers placed on the clips in Final Cut Pro. In addition, still frames can be exported from the clip's QuickTime files based on markers and the QuickTime's Finder-level poster frames can be set.

XMiL Songster: Drag your AIFF, WAVE or MP3 files to the XMiL Songster icon, and it will create an XML document that includes the metadata from the files' ID3 tags. It shoots that XML right into Final Cut Pro and the clips will appear automatically in a new

---

[216] http://www.AssistedEditing.com/

[217] http://xmil.biz/

untitled project. XMiL Songster ALE is a very similar application that produces Avid ALE files instead of Final Cut Pro XML.

XMiL Sequencer converts a XML file exported from a Final Cut Pro timeline and turns it into an Avid Log Exchange (ALE) file. This file can then be imported into an Avid nonlinear editing system, turning the segments used in the FCP timeline into Avid master clips.

XMiL Copier simply copies files from one folder to another, watching for new files to appear in the origin folder. It's useful for overnight exports of big files that you want in two different locations when you come in the next morning. XMiL Copier works with applications like Final Cut Pro, Avid or After Effects, and it can put copies of the exported files on an external drive for delivery to someone else.

Spherico[218]

TCR Plus is a simple to use utility, which allows a better and faster way for review and approval of cuts. It combines FCP's XML power with a FCP plug-in .

TextUp Pro and TextUp are FCP plugins/generators, which are especially useful for subtitles.

TitleExchange Pro for FCP is a basic tool for easy and fast transfer of subtitles from FCP to DVD Studio Pro. There is a great tutorial on DVD Studio and subtitles at Ripple Training[219] (done by Steve Martin).

textViewer is simply a free tool which allows to view and modify STL text subtitles for DVD Studio Pro. It will also display right to left reading languages in a way we expect.

TitleCleaner is a tool, which makes use of the Final Cut Pro XMLs to clean text from subtitles much easier and faster than it can be done within FCP. It also allows to use the native OS X spell checker or some third party tools like Ultralingual.

markerTool is a small freeware which allows to shuffle around markers in FCP sequences

---

[218] http://www.spherico.com/filmtools/

[219] http://www.rippletraining.com/movies/Free Downloads/ dvdsp_subsanity_960.mov

sequenceLiner is beta software which allows you to lay down clips to a pre-defined sequence according to their Timecodes.

readXML reads FCP XML files. You can load any kind of XML from FCP, but only clips or sequences will be parsed dependent upon the user's choice what to process.

BWF2XML allows you to transport metadata from Broadcast Wave Format files into FCP. This version is especially thought for QT 7 and FCP 5.

SoundCount is the fast and easy way to calculate the total playtime of commercial sound in a sequence or project. SoundCount is a big timesaver if you are working with commercial sounds.

rotateClips: A small helper application for people using the 35mm adapter with their camera. It allows to either "Flop" all clips in a project or rotate them in one single step – more than 2500 clips in a 64MB XML were changed in about 10 seconds, where loading the XML into memory and writing it back to disk took most of the time.

XML4Dailies: The easy way to bring some subtitling for dailies into FCP or DVD Studio Pro. Export your sequence to a XML file, convert it with XML4Dailies, bring it back into FCP just with a double click and you are ready to go. For DVD Studio Pro you get STL files and a chapter marker list. The new version allows better control of the XML output, i.e. the appearance of the titles in FCP.

Free Plugins for FCP: **Basic Text:** a simple modification of the original 'Lower 3rd' text generator. It has additional controls for horizontal and vertical position of the text, as well as text alignment. **Jiggler** is a simple effect which jiggles the position of the frame randomly.

Playlist2FCP completely automates the transfer of audio tracks from iTunes to FCP. By leveraging the power of the FCP XML format, Playlist2FCP allows FCP to seamlessly import iTunes Playlists, complete with Track Name, Artist and Album information into FCP.

Video Toolshed[220]

ALE cleaner: A simple program to make batch redigitizing of decomposed sequences way faster.

autoFTP is a utility that watches a directory and will upload new files that appear there to your FTP server. If you want it, AutoFTP generates HTML for fast starting movies and upload the HTML too.

Avid Locator to DVD chapter converter: To convert Avid Locators to Chapter Markers for DVD SP, export images and Cinemacraft marker lists.

Deck control: This is a multiple deck controller for RS-422 devices. It can control up to 9 decks in its current state.

EDL Tool: Free utility to make changes in multicam EDLs or mirror EDLs for color correction on edited masters

FCP auxTC reader: Util to automatically read and add AUX TC from LTC on one of the audio channels to a real FCP aux TC Timecode track. It is now in 1.3.0, and can merge BWF files with the corresponding QT video files.

FCP text generator: A plugin for Final Cut Pro, giving your decent text. Controllable by XML trough Subbits. Free.

LiveCut: A live switching recorder. With a connection to the tally system of the switcher you can create EDL's to have an easy edit when using a lot of ISOs

LTC logger: Easy way to log clips from your camera or deck. It can detect camera stops while you're shooting, or find tc breaks. Either way, it can work unattended if you want it. No additional hardware required, just an audio input on your computer.

LTC reader: A simple utility that can display timecode on your computer and put it into any application with just a keystroke.

Proxyrenderer: Extremely fast transcoding to H264, Mpeg4, Mpeg1 and MJPEG, with de-interlacing, customizable crop and scaling. It also creates HTML, so you can have your client

---

[220] http://www.videotoolshed.com/?page=products

previews up in no time. Just set your parameters once, then just drag and drop your files.

ReCut: A fast scene/shot detector, The perfect addition for your NLE or Color correction tools.

rs422 / File Logger: A fast and handy 422 and File logger.

Saver: A little utility that makes backups of your file, while you're working on them.

SCCoffset: A utility to view captions before authoring, and (if you like) make an offset in a scenarist CC file. It doubles as a Mpeg-2 Elementary stream / AC3 player, and gives you readable text instead of the funny words you find in the file if you open it with a text editor.

SubBits subtitler: The ultimate subtitle editor/generator. Edit, time and generate subtitles for output to video, DVD or broadcast. Latest update: QuickTime Timecode support, VEC foot-pedal support for both Windows/Macintosh, Avid SubCap support, Timed Text / Flash XML and Closed Caption support.

Transcriber 2 DVD: Background Media Player with QuickTime Timecode reading, BWF Timecode reading and file based LTC reading. Have control over your audio/video within any application, and paste the current TC in your document. All without leaving your program of choice! Now with foot-pedal support.

Video Assist assist: This utility reads VITC in captured clips and renames and trims them to values from an external database. And no, the name is not misspelled.

VideoMacro: A utility that runs user-definable macros, specially designed for non-linear editors. Euro 9.95

VITC reader: Free small mediaplayer that can read VITC timecode from digitized clips, and reads header info from Mpeg I or Mpeg II files.

Edit Groove [221]

UserMatic – a powerful Preferences chooser (multiple users) for Final Cut Pro.

---

[221] http://www.editgroove.com/

Handmade Digital[222]

VFX Tracker 2008 – a simple solution to tracking visual effects across multiple versions within Final Cut Pro. XMiL Placer complements this application and shares its VFXINFO filter.

MetaLabPro[223]

MetaLabPro – a Microsoft Excel-based solution for handling all time code, keycode, scanning and cut data of film and video projects

Get Paid Faster

One of the first signs of a down economy is that good payers end up slowing down payments to vendors. If you're already experiencing customer payment slowdown, these five tips will help. If you're fortunate enough to not yet have your customers payments stretch out to the third or fourth month, these tips will help prevent it happening.

Never feel reluctant to invoice customers. You have done great work for them, helping make them more money (or you don't have a future) so there's no reason to feel the slightest bit embarrassed about wanting to be paid, and paid promptly.

Pay Fast

Let's consider the other side of the equation: if you want to be paid fast, pay fast yourself. Unless you never want to do business with a supplier or subcontractor again, keep the relationship good by paying when due, or ahead of when due. Doing so will keep the business relationship alive and improve your reputation. You'll become a valued client of theirs and get preferential treatment if it ever comes down to a choice of doing business with you, or with someone else.

---

[222] http://www.vfxtracker.net/

[223] http://metalabpro.com/

You are not a bank –
reset your status with customers

If you find yourself getting strung out for payment then you need to reset the relationship. If necessary, go to those customers who are slowing payment and say something like:

> "I'm sure you'll agree that we're very good at improving your business communication with our services and we appreciate your business, but I feel I need to point out that we're a production (or postproduction) business and not a bank. If we were a bank we'd probably be getting a great fat bailout but we're not and I'm going to have to ask you to stop treating us like an overdraft facility, or unfortunately we're not going to be able to continue to help you achieve your business goals."

Make sure you make it clear you'll run through hoops for the customer but you expect them to pay in a timely manner.

You'll appreciate working with clients that appreciate you and show it by paying promptly.

> **Tip for the Paranoid:** Watermark all preview tapes, DVDs or files before payment has been received. I once had the misfortune of a customer taking their review VHS tape and duplicating that to avoid paying me for the work they clearly accepted.

Talk about payment terms up front

You're going to have to talk about it sometime and before you're committed to the work is the best time. Unless payment terms are part of the agreement, customers can always claim they "didn't know" or "we can't do that". If there is a genuine problem that their company cannot pay on your terms, this is the time to negotiate it, not when the job is complete.

Know your profitable customers

Do you know how much each client's payment cycle costs you?

In a post at Howard Mann's Business Brickyard, Colleen Barrett – former President of Southwest Airlines – has this story[224] to tell about examining the profitability of each customer based in part on payment history.

> "Years ago, we created a simple spreadsheet that showed how much we earned from each client in the past year, how much time they took to pay us and what that cost us using the current interest rate. Some of those spreadsheets were an eye opener to say the least. We had clients that were costing us 30% of our profit in interest. We brought the spreadsheets to our clients and had a fair and honest business conversation. It provoked discussions about why they paid slowly and we learned about things we could do that made our invoices easier to process. It never turned into a negative."

Send your invoice promptly

In a small production or postproduction business, it's the video work that interests most of us. The fact that we have to run a business as well is kind of a drag. One consequence is that invoices don't get sent out promptly. Realistically you can't expect anyone to pay until they have the invoice, so get the invoice out the door as quickly after the client accepts the work as possible.

> **Important:** I'm talking about tried and true customers here. If you're working with a totally new customer stick to the traditional policy of 30% payment of budget when work commences; 30% at the completion of production (or suitable postproduction milestone, like first draft assembly) and the balance of 40% due on completion. For new customers it's very unwise to let the master out to the customer until payment has been made (and cleared the bank).

---

[224] http://businessbrickyard.com/blog/2008/11/5-ways-to-get-paid-faster

Avoid the mail

Once you let the postal system have control over your invoice you don't know when it was received unless you take out receipt confirmation, which requires a trip to the post office for each invoice. Not fun. Instead, email the invoice and ask the client to confirm receipt. If you don't hear back within a day or so, follow up with another email or phone call to confirm that the invoice has been received and that there are no problems with it.

Send them a PDF, Word document or use an online service to invoice. (Freshbooks[225] or Blinksale[226] are 2 online options that people are using and that will work well. Billings[227] is a good option for Mac users.)

> **Problems**: Should a client suggest they have a problem with the invoice it's better to find out as quickly as possible. If there is a genuine technical or other issue that can be corrected, correct it. Usually it's not so straightforward and a client is disputing whether or not they authorized additional work, or whatever. This is where you'll be very thankful that you have a written agreement in place, which states the payment terms and scope of work and have signed authorizations for work beyond that original scope.

Know the client's payment process

The larger the company, the more complicated getting paid is. Know their system so you can work with it to your advantage, or at least not make payment unnecessarily slow because of a mistake at your end.

Most companies will require that you have an official purchase order number on every invoice. You should have that before you start work. Make sure that all required numbers – Purchase Order number; department number, job number, quote number, etc – are on the invoice. I always find it useful to include a copy of the purchase order with the invoice – it makes it hard to "be confused".

---

[225] http://www.freshbooks.com/

[226] http://www.blinksale.com/home

[227] http://www.billingsapp.com/

Offer a discount

Depending on your jurisdiction many Utilities and Government bodies are legally obliged to take advantage of any discounts offered. I had considerable success back in Australia by offering a 1% discount for 14 day terms. Once that offer was made, a whole class of client were legally mandated to pay within 14 days, and a quick phone call reminding the head of the payments department of their legal obligation always shook out the payment immediately.

Make your invoices pleasant

Invoices are a fact of life but make them appealing. Get the person who designed your logo and stationary to design the invoice. Make it look attractive and look like your company.

If you have a relatively small number of customers, like we typically do in production and postproduction, then take the time to write a personal message with the invoice (in the email or an accompanying letter). Make it some funny quote, or poignant statement about the industry, or something relevant to the customer's business. By including something pleasant you can eventually make people look forward to your invoice. It can be the same message on every invoice, although change it at least every month.

If the shear numbers of invoices makes it difficult to add a personal note (and I envy you this problem) even a generic "thanks for entrusting us with the work, it's been great helping you achieve your goals" message. Colleen Barrett again, from the same article:

> "Even a variety of facts about your company or staff works. Make it memorable and make it work with the personality of your business. I had one vendor who mentioned in their invoice when staff members had a birthday or had a baby, which drove home their family oriented nature."

Systematically follow up every invoice

This is such good advice, and I'm personally so bad at it that I'm almost embarrassed to include it. But it's true: we need to have a systematic follow-up for every invoice if we want to be paid promptly.

Simply sending out a 'Past Due' notice and subsequent monthly statements isn't going to cause a company deliberately delaying payment any stress or pressure. We're enabling their poor behavior!

You have both agreed on the payment schedule, so email or call just before the payment's due as a gentle reminder. Frame this in a positive way: "just a friendly reminder that we're expecting payment on xyz invoice so we can meet our obligations. I just wanted to check that everything is on schedule."

Never let copyright pass until you're paid in full

One of the things I learnt from the client I mentioned at the start of this section, who had taken the review copy and duplicated from that, was to put a clause in the agreement (never a contract, that scares people) such that copyright in the work did not pass to the client until payment was received in full.

This became very helpful a few years later when I worked on a music video for a band signed to one of the four major record labels. Payment was very late from the record company and they seemed rather disinclined to change that any time soon. (This was now 90 days from invoice.)

Having made a decision I didn't want to work with these people again, I called the record company's accounts payable department, who again declined to be helpful, so I simply asked to be transferred to legal. That spurred their interest! I pointed out that they did not yet have copyright clearance in the music video, and their use of it on a couple of (Australian) national music TV shows was a breach of my copyright and I wanted to start proceedings.

I had the check delivered 48 hours later without a word to legal.

It's a blunt instrument, and only really useful when the relationship has broken down and future work is unlikely, but it ups the ante because willful breach of copyright has penalties attached that inadvertent breaching does not.

12: Find your own income

Early in 2009, I wrote a <u>blog post on the role of failure</u>[228], or near miss, on innovation. Well, during the 1990's my production company had "significant excess capacity" or in plain terms, we were not really that busy. Coincidentally, around that time I discovered an opportunity making videos for basic metal trade skills.

I wish I could claim that it came to me in a brilliant flash of insight, but reality is that the idea came up almost by accident. It did sustain the company through quiet periods over the balance of the 1980's and into the mid 1990's.

The idea was a simple one: produce videos to go with existing curriculum, taught at around 75 Tertiary and Further Education (TAFE) colleges around Australia. (TAFE colleges are somewhat similar to Community Colleges in the USA.) There wasn't a central body of funding for these, but there was a ready market for 50-60 of each title, if the video was produced. That was where we came in!

How it came about

During most of my career I have taught video production at tertiary level and two of my students were in charge of training apprentices at local industries – big enough to have in-house apprentice training facilities. They told us about the national curriculum for basic metal trades and that there were no educational resources beyond the manual produced for the national curriculum.

After their initial attempts at production were disappointing we came to the understanding that we would produce the video; the facility we used would get a free copy of the video; the facility would provide the tools and examples necessary and the location for filming.

We provided script production, postproduction and distribution and I found a local professional actor who was great at playing an ordinary guy. His performance was consistent across the day and between memorized and read pieces. He had a terrific short-term

---

[228] http://www.philiphodgetts.com/?p=224

memory so no autocue was required. Each video took 2-4 days to shoot and a couple of weeks to post because of the animation and graphics required.

We never sold fewer than 52 copies, generally in the high 60's and each production returned us a profit of about Au$10-15,000. Not necessarily huge money, but enough to keep the lights on when external clients were between projects!

Business structure

In our case we created a separate corporation to handle commissioning, marketing and sales of these productions. That corporation commissioned our production company to produce the video and paid for it with the income from sales.

This worked very well for bringing the production work to book, improving the overall figures for both companies. However, I'm told this structure may not be valid in the USA, so check with your accountant if you want to go down that path.

Other opportunities

From that accidental beginning we began to see other opportunities. We built the videos into "training packages" by adding teacher guides and student worksheets – even for those that had national curriculum behind then – because the worksheets and guides were perceived added value that allowed us to double the original prices for video alone.

We did not lose a single sale.

Eventually we started partnering with our own clients. On one project for the Coal Association (industry body of coal mine owners) I suggested we pick up 1/3 of the cost of production but shoot a generic industry version while shooting the coal-industry specific version of a project on Drugs and Alcohol in the workplace. We additionally shot a version for office workers with different drug-related issues.

We did something similar with another training package encouraging injured workers back to the workplace (on alternate duties if necessary) where we did a version for the coal industry, who commissioned the project, but also shot a more generic version while we were on location so we could cut an alternate release for our own marketing company.

That training package remains one of my finest pieces of work, both as a piece of quality video but also as a piece of quality training.

We also partnered with trainers, State funding and industry bodies to create an 8 hours food handling safety-training package that contained only 1.5 hours of video material. In return for our work, we received some State funding but mostly from the sales of the package to restaurants and cooking schools.

The value of owning content

Content that you own and continue to sell is the gift that keeps on giving. If you can use some down time to produce video that you can turn into a revenue stream, then you take one further step to making your business recession-proof and being in control of your own destiny.

Projects that you own do add a marketing burden, but the principles I've outlined in this book for promoting your business work equally well, if not better, for an independently produced entertainment or educational project.

The only type of content that does not seem to be valuable to own is an independent feature or short, which seem to mostly languish without audience or distribution. Smart producers, like Tiffany Shlain[229], producer/director of *The Tribe* and *Connected* (and the founder of the Webby Awards) and Mike Shiley [230] have made great use of the new approaches PR and social media to make their documentaries financially (and creatively) successful.

There is one additional value to owning content: you can sell it at some future time. We sold the copywrite of several of the training packages to other companies in those training areas.

---

[229] http://www.tiffanyshlain.com/Home.html

[230] http://www.shidogfilms.com/

Where are the opportunities?

Local markets are finite and it can be hard to aggregate a market that is big enough to make the return worthwhile. Thanks to the Internet we don't have to be limited to local markets. The market for the *Media 100 Editor's Companion* publication in my local market was exactly four copies. Worldwide we did about 1000 sales, which made the project very worthwhile.

It is thanks to the Internet – part of the New Now – that we can contemplate projects that would never have been financially viable can now aggregate markets big enough to be profitable.

The ideal topic

The ideal candidate for an independent revenue stream from your own production is one where:

1. There is an identifiable market, preferably already with some community attached;

2. There is an ongoing opportunity to create compelling programming;

3. There is little or no other video being produced to meet this need;

4. Production is not going to risk your business; and

5. It's something you know about or care deeply about and bring passion to the project.

Even if all five conditions are not met you can still contemplate a project as long as condition four *is* met.

Identifiable Market

Almost every topic in the world has some identifiable group, trade body or user community. These are the clues to finding markets. Whether it's a group of Community Colleges all desperate for teaching resources on common curriculum, or places that prepare food, these are identifiable groups relatively easy to reach.

As well as online communities also look to special interest magazines as a possible source of inspiration as a marketing partner.

Ongoing opportunity

A one-off project is definitely worth considering, but the ideal project has the opportunity for ongoing production and sale of content. Technique videos, travel, sport techniques, hobby, etc, all have lots of potential topics.

With multiple topics you can spread out the community building and marketing/PR efforts over multiple titles. Each time we produce a new PDF book title, we first offer it to previous customers (at a discount) therefore leveraging previous work to a current project.

One notable exception to the ongoing opportunity is video for "disease" sufferers. While these have usually resulted from a personal connection to a sufferer of the disease, DVDs on "Coping with my malaise" sell consistently as more people are diagnosed with the disease. These DVDs can be very profitable and provide useful source of information to people at a difficult time.

Little or no content already produced

With the cost of production dropping so dramatically over the last decade, people have jumped into what are perceived as the most popular titles, because they have big potential markets. So the chance of success with another golfing video might not be anywhere near as high as a series on porcelain plate overglaze techniques.

Google is your friend. Search as if you were trying to buy video or DVD on the topic. If you find plenty, look elsewhere for your opportunity.

Don't risk the company

The great thing about the metal trades skills video that I discussed at the start of this section, is that they required very little pay-out. We paid the talent the going professional day rate, which was just Au$300 at the time, for 2-4 days per production. A cameraman and assistant/audio person rounded out the crew with me as writer/director/editor/graphics. I invested substantial time, for sure, but very little cash. We produced each for less than Au$2,000 out-of-pocket expenses. Since there was no other work offering at the time (and the production of these projects could be shuffled around more commercial opportunities) this was time well invested.

Do not take on a project that **must** be successful or you risk your financial future. This is a problem with too many independent features that you do not want to emulate.

It's a gamble: spend as much as you can afford to lose, no more.

Be passionate about the project

While being passionate about the income is probably the primary passion in evidence here, you should definitely have affinity for the topic, preferably one you know something about.

Your passion for the content will drive your marketing into that community, where you'll be an equal, not a "marketing gatecrasher"!

Examples

There are a million examples but these few come from my own experience, or that of my friends and associates.

This is the Hunter

As we developed the idea of independent projects we owned, I had the idea of creating a "video postcard" about the region we lived in. To the best of my knowledge this was the first time it was done anywhere in the world. It wasn't a travelogue video but rather a visual feast like a series of moving postcards showing off the Hunter Region of NSW, Australia.

The initial release had no voice-over at all, just a well mixed music and effects bed. This was too radical for most people and (under protest) I added minimal narration at the top of each section.

TripFLIX

Fellow International Media User Group[231] member Dave Bittner and his wife Ilana created TripFLIX[232] to take advantage of in-car DVD systems to create an engaging, interactive educational media piece for kids that let them choose their own adventure, from coast to coast.

---

[231] http://www.imugonline.com/

[232] http://www.tripflix.com

This project is separate from their production business, Pixel Workshop.

It took two years of development, a year of shooting some of the most interesting and quirky locations in the continental USA, and hundreds of hours of editing and programming to get to the point they are now: an independent business.

I doubt TripFLIX would have been as easy to build if they'd had to pay full commercial rates for production before any revenue flowed.

Porcelain Plate Overglaze training

In the mid 1980's I acquired a client in Sydney, to produce videos showing techniques on how to paint an overglaze image on porcelain plates.

Apart from being a most challenging assignment because there could be no shadows or reflections on the concave, shiny plate, it was obvious that this couple had found a very successful niche for themselves.

They already published a magazine, distributed worldwide, for porcelain plate painters, and supplied the powders and blank plates hobbyists needed, so adding training videos to the mix made perfect sense.

Clearly they were successful in their niche by surface measures: they lived in a very large home in a very, very expensive area of Sydney with expensive furnishings in the house and expensive cars in the driveway.

Wonderful World of Flying

Steve Kahn of Edit on Hudson[233] worked with ABC Television in the mid-80's on the production of the *Wonderful World of Flying* series. Steve's production company retained the rights to the video after the television run and still, more than 20 years later, the DVDs and digital downloads[234] are still selling.

---

[233] http://www.editonhudson.com/

[234] http://www.wwof.com/

HD Survival Handbook, this book

The perfect place to finish this section, and the book, is to point out that my *HD Survival Handbook*[235] and this book, *The New Now*, are both independent projects that we retained the copyright to. While, at the time of writing, I don't know how well this book will do, *The HD Survival Handbook* has returned more profit as an independent project than it would have if it had been published through more traditional publishing channels, with a publisher heading the project.

Services like Amazon's CreateSpace[236] mean that this book is available in both digital download and physical form. Each form will return way more per book than the commission from a publisher.

If ever we go back to independent video production – and we will if the right opportunity arises – I'll be making it available through the Open TV Network's klickTab[237] service.

Take control of your future by creating content you own and distribute yourself so you retain all the profit. The barriers to independent distribution have fallen with the advent of the Internet and the techniques we've been discussing in this book. Do it now!

---

[235] http://www.proappstips.com/HDSurvivalHandbook/

[236] https://www.createspace.com/

[237] http://www.klickTab.com

3940070